The ABC's
of
Christian Faith

The ABC's
of
Christian Faith

by
JAMES D. SMART

THE WESTMINSTER PRESS
Philadelphia

LIBRARY OF CONGRESS CATALOG CARD NO. 68–13958

Published by The Westminster Press ®
Philadelphia, Pennsylvania

PRINTED IN THE UNITED STATES OF AMERICA

Contents

Preface

THIS BOOK is written for the general reader who finds himself frustrated by what he hears concerning the Christian faith and has begun to be aware that there is a considerable degree of confusion in the way certain key words are used. There has been no attempt to define all the key words. That would have required a much larger book, in fact nothing less than a theological dictionary of the Bible and of the Christian faith. Readers will be likely to think at once of words each of which should have been made the subject of a chapter: thanksgiving, prayer, Baptism, Eucharist, Spirit, death, sacrifice, service, etc. But a large book would defeat the very purpose for which this one was first conceived: to show the interested layman that the Christian gospel opens up to him in a new way when he gives to the key words their original meaning, and to suggest to preachers and teachers the task of redefinition which they must undertake if they would expect to be understood.

I owe a debt of thanks to my friend, David K. Perrie, of Elmvale, Ontario, for a careful reading of the manuscript and valuable suggestions to improve its clarity for the general public.

J. D. S.

Bala, Ontario, Canada
August, 1967

1

A Breakdown
in Communication

MANY YEARS AGO one of my daughters began to have serious difficulty with her arithmetic lessons in school. It was clear that the problem lay not in her intelligence or in the complexity of the lessons. A brief investigation disclosed that she had never properly learned her multiplication tables, one of the ABC's of arithmetic. The defect, once detected, could be soon remedied. The same principle holds true in every realm of knowledge and understanding — confusion at any point in the first elements of the subject can cause a breakdown in communication and a paralysis of understanding at some later stage. However, the defect may not be so easily remedied.

The complaint is heard frequently today that those who speak for the Christian church, whether preachers or teachers, are guilty of using a language that does not make sense to the hearers. What is disturbing is that the complaint comes most often not from the unintelligent and thoughtless but from the most thoughtful and intelligent attenders of our churches. Again and again they come away frustrated, confessing, " It just didn't say anything to me." When the preaching or teaching is the product of incompetence, a hodgepodge of inherited religious phrases, roughly set together to form some kind of pattern, welded to one another chiefly by emotion rather than by any logical connection, and ornamented with illustrations which hold the interest but fail to carry forward any line of thought, the frustration is inevitable. But when the frustration occurs in response to preaching and teaching in which at least a serious attempt is being made to present the Christian gospel in terms that are relevant and intelligible for modern man, we should be warned that something has gone wrong with the words that we are using as our means of communication. What is being spoken is no longer being heard. The words have ceased to convey their proper burden of meaning, and the result is a breakdown in communication.

Words are the ABC's in this realm of communication. Far too quickly do we assume that words have a fixed meaning, like a standard coinage in which a coin has the same value whoever may be handling it. Some words do have a reasonably fixed value, especially when they refer to tangible objects — a door, a tree, a rosebush. But as soon as we begin to use words to describe the intangible we find ourselves in difficulty. " Justice," " truth," " freedom," are words that point to realities fundamental to our existence, but humanity today is sharply divided, and perhaps subdivided, in its definition of them. " Freedom " to a Communist is one thing; to a rugged individualist it is something quite different; and in the New Testament it is something else again. " Justice " in the State of Alabama seems to be not quite the same as " justice " in the Commonwealth of Pennsylvania. And one hardly needs to point out that this difference in the meaning of words is not a surface phenomenon but reflects a difference in basic convictions and in the whole orientation of life that constitutes a dangerous barrier between man and man. When there begin to be confusion and contradiction in men's definitions of freedom and justice, the consequences for human society are likely to be serious.

Communication depends upon some measure of common understanding of the meaning of words, that is, some measure of agreement in defining the intangible realities to which the words refer. If certain key words have different meanings in the minds of two people who are conversing, they will find themselves talking past each other instead of to each other. What is spoken will not be what is heard, because the meaning of the words in the context of the speaker's mind is not the same as the meaning of the words in the context of the hearer's mind. One of the most vivid instances of this is what happens when a congregation hears in the Scripture lesson the Beatitude, " Blessed are the meek, for they shall inherit the earth." The word " meek " in Jesus' usage of it means " one who is utterly humbled before God." It has to do with that central humbling of the human self in which a man is freed of his self-centeredness so that in radical openness to God he may be unconditionally open also to his fellowman. It is the very basis not only of a right relationship with God but also of strong wholesome relationships in men's dealings with one another. But what does the word " meek " signify to most of the listeners? To them a meek person is one who weakly lets others ride over him, quickly giving way in the face of opposition, a person who makes himself a doormat for his fellowmen. Therefore, in the Beatitude they hear Jesus inviting them to be weaklings of this kind and promising the world and all that is in it to such Caspar Milquetoasts. One such word, wrongly defined, can introduce a serious confusion into the hearer's conception of the Christian faith.

During the past thirty-six years I have been concerned with this problem of communication as preacher, teacher, editor of educational literature, and professor of theology, and I have had nearly as many years' experience as a listener in church as I have had in the pulpit. At the beginning and for many years thereafter, I assumed that if I prepared my sermon or lesson with care so that it said something distinctly and convincingly to me, it would speak in the same way to any attentive hearer. Eventually I learned the fallacy of this, but it took some sad and shocking experiences to convince me. It is distressing to have a person thank you for something in a sermon which you know you never said, so that in bewilderment you have to check that it really was *your* sermon the person heard. It is much more distressing to find that after years of what seemed to be earnest and sympathetic listening to your preaching, people are completely ignorant and unmoved at the very points that to you were most central and decisive for the understanding and the living out of the Christian gospel. They listened but they did not hear. One's first impulse is to blame the listener. His earnest attentiveness concealed an actual unconcern, a closed mind! Reflection, however, suggests a much deeper problem and a humbler and more compassionate attitude. Speaker and hearers alike are involved in the dilemma.

The problem has levels which we shall not be able to explore here with any thoroughness. (The next two paragraphs may trip up the general reader. They may be skipped by him without undue loss — but not by preachers or teachers.) There is the relativity and transitoriness of everything human, including the concepts and the language in which we express our deepest convictions. We rebel against it and try to absolutize the order of life and language that most appeals to us at some one moment. But when we do, we merely condemn ourselves to stagnation and to speaking a language that has lost much of its meaning. Our words, like so much else, have to die and be reborn. Hence we have had, and always shall have in the church, a succession of schools of theology and no one of them can ever have the last word. One has continually to say things in a new way in order to be saying even what one meant to say before.

Again, there is the problem of translation that every preacher and teacher has to face, not just the translation of Christian truth from its Hebrew and Greek forms of expression, which is complex enough, but also the translation of one's own understanding of Christian truth from the specialized language of academic theology into the language of ordinary men, women, and children. Failure at either of these points can cause a breakdown in communication.

A third aspect of the problem concerns speaker and hearer alike. Christian truth is not a body of intellectual knowledge that can be conveyed from one person to the other merely by the speaking and hearing of words. The kind of knowing with which we are concerned here compasses the whole of one's existence. The truth is a life, a life in personal relationship with God and with our fellowmen. The words spoken, therefore, are witness to that life in both dimensions and have meaning for the hearer only in the measure that he recognizes that life as his own life. To know God is the goal of all the speaking, but to know God is to be possessed, sustained, fulfilled, and enlightened by God himself. Our hearing, thus, can reach its goal only when the words spoken somehow point us beyond themselves to the living present reality of the God who in each moment seeks our good and is ever more ready to be known by us than we are to know him. The words of themselves cannot do what we expect them to do. They cannot give us God or the life in God which is our only true life. They can only point us to that narrow pass in which God himself meets us and deals with us.

All these aspects of our problem are in the background of our present discussion, but it has a more limited scope. We are concerned only with the ABC's, that is, with the meaning of a number of key words without which we are unable to say anything about the Christian faith, words such as " gospel," " conversion," " faith," " sin," " Christ," " God." The assumption is generally made by preacher, teacher, and people, all alike, that these basic words have an obvious meaning and can be used without further definition. But the situation is very much like that of the arithmetic teacher who assumed that all her pupils had memorized the multiplication tables. Many of these key words have in our time taken on meanings that are quite different from those which they have in their Biblical context, or they have become vague and shadowy in men's minds. They cease then to be bearers of their true meaning. One of the primary tasks of theological education is the defining of terms, the restoration of their true meaning to the words we use, but the labor is wasted unless the same task is undertaken in the education of Christians in general.

There is reason to think that this task is very widely neglected. Who wants to be put back into the kindergarten to learn his ABC's afresh? Yet when one frequently comes upon intelligent, earnest people who have been alienated from the church by what are flagrant misconceptions of sin and salvation, or who confess that in spite of all their efforts they cannot grasp what the preacher is talking about, it suggests that preacher and people alike may need to reexamine the ABC's of the Christian faith. In fact, this may be part of what Jesus meant when he said that we have to become as little children if we would enter the Kingdom of God — that it belongs to the nature of the realities with which we are concerned in the Christian life that we can never take the simplest elements, the ABC's, for granted, but have again and again to return to the spiritual kindergarten and spell them out afresh.

2
Life

WHERE SHALL WE BEGIN? Where is the *A* of the Christian alphabet? Begin with God, say some, for until there is a firm belief in God you can get nowhere. And it sounds reasonably convincing. Must not God always be first? Does not the Creed begin, " I believe in God "? Is not the chief difficulty of vast numbers of people today, not only in the world at large but also in the church itself, that they have become either vague and uncertain or completely negative about God? What is more striking in the present religious scene than the existence of men who still call themselves Christian theologians and yet profess to be no longer able to believe in God? Therefore, for some the first step would be an attempt to make belief in God credible for modern men. The difficulty with this is that there is nothing specifically Christian about believing in God. It has been true through the ages that the very bulwark of an antichristian faith may be a belief in God. The men who sent Jesus to his death believed firmly in God.

Begin with Jesus Christ, say others, for he is the center from which all things in the Christian faith must be understood. There is little to be said against this. We shall find how true it is as we proceed. However, it could mean beginning at a point where many readers are not yet involved. The words " Jesus Christ " still mean for them a person who lived a long time ago, the founder of the Christian faith. We need a word that involves *both* him and us, a

word that brings *both* him and every one of us upon the
scene. And that word is " life."

The hunger for life is something that everyone knows. It
is inescapable. It begins very early as a person becomes
conscious of a contradiction between what he is and what
he might be. There are moments in which he feels more
truly himself than at other times, but such moments are
fleeting and may leave him restless and dissatisfied in the
long stretches of his time. He recognizes the contrast between the times in which he is " not himself " and the moments of self-realization, but he is driven to despair by
his inability to make the self of those precious moments
endure. This consciousness of a contradiction in oneself
between " alive " and " not alive " is matched by the consciousness of a similar contradiction beyond oneself in human society, between life that is being fulfilled and life
that is stunted, broken, suppressed, denied. Here is the
central problem of our world: how men are to be set free
to live, to be themselves in the fullest and truest sense. The
hunger for one's own life thus broadens out to become a
passionate hunger for life on behalf of all men.

This hunger for life can have both superficial and profound expressions. It is pathetic when it exhausts itself in
grasping at experiences which merely make one " feel
alive " for the few moments that the experience lasts, or
lets itself be subdued by an accumulation of possessions.
But it can be the driving force that sends men forth from
their limited beginnings to explore the possibilities of life
in the diverse realms of human culture and experience. A
cow is content with the grass in the field and the warmth
of its stall. That is its life. Man, however, is tortured by a
discontent that constantly makes him seek his life beyond
the established order of his world. In his hunger for life he
develops science, literature, and art and builds himself civilizations, and then the same hunger breaks forth in revo-
lutions against the unjust order imposed upon him by his

civilizations. He seeks a world and a life that constantly elude him.

Corresponding to this universal hunger for life is the offer of life which is at the heart of a Biblical faith. Early in the Old Testament, God is represented as saying, " Behold, I set before you the way of life and the way of death." The offer was addressed not to individuals but to a community. The words " life " and " death " are used not to signify existence and nonexistence but rather existence with a future in which life moves toward its fulfillment and existence that has no future. The same offer is made by the prophet Amos on God's behalf: " Seek ye me and live," where " seeking God " means standing in a relation with him in which his will to justice and righteousness is reflected in the life of the community. The whole Old Testament is a setting forth of the two ways, first for the community and then later for the individual, drawing a line sharply between a life that is no better than death and has no prospect but death and a life that can be lived with confidence, hope, and thankfulness because it has in it the promise of fulfillment. Life, it is insisted, is not something a man can have in himself alone. He has it only in covenant with God, that is, in a relationship of openness and faithfulness toward God, reflecting the very nature of God, and only in solidarity with his brothers.

So also in the New Testament the offer of life is central. The Fourth Gospel grasps this firmly when it describes the purpose of Jesus' coming as the abolition of death and the opening to all men of an abundant life. Here again " death " is a kind of existence rather than a ceasing to exist, existence in darkness rather than in the light, and " life " is a kind of existence that is possible only as " life in God," in which the very life of God himself, eternal life, becomes the life of man. The same Gospel portrays Jesus as possessing that " life " in himself and having as his unique power the ability to communicate it to other men. The same tension between two kinds of existence is expressed in Jesus' teaching in the other three Gospels when he contrasts life in the Kingdom of God with the present life of men. The Kingdom, from far back in the Old Testament, is an envisioning of what life will be for man when it reaches its fulfillment. Jesus announced that the hour of fulfillment was no longer distant but was immediately at hand. The nearness of the Kingdom was the nearness of God and of a new life in the presence and power of God. Some scholars have thought that Jesus gave men only a more intense expectation of the coming of the Kingdom in the future, but this ignores not only Jesus' claim that the time of fulfillment was come but also the evidence of life-transforming power being present in the person of Jesus himself and being communicated through him to his followers. The aim of Jesus' mission was to set men free for their true life in fellowship with God and man.

One thing needs to be made very clear: what both Old and New Testaments call " life " is not some special kind of religious life or life in a world other than the one we now inhabit. One of the services of the Old Testament to our faith is to make this very emphatic. The Old Testament is focused almost entirely on life in this world, life in human society, with only late glimmerings of a life beyond the grave. For Israel to live is for the community to find an enduring realization of its existence in an order in which justice and mercy prevail. It is a life that is spelled out primarily in the social, economic, and political relationships of the people. For the prophet, the test of the nation's relationship with God is how men are dealing with one another in the secular life of the community.

It is easier and commoner for the New Testament use of the word " life " to be misrepresented. There is a tradition that makes of it a " spiritual life," a " life of the soul " in contrast to life in the world. Jesus had only a spiritual mission, they say; he had no concern with the social, economic, and political problems of men. The fact that the Fourth Gospel calls the life Jesus offers to men " eternal life " is made the basis for contrasting it with our life in time. But the adjective " eternal " is meant only to say that a life in fellowship with God is beyond the reach of death, and not in any way to deny that it is the fulfillment of life in the human community on earth. Usually the so-called " spiritual life " turns out to be a very rigidly defined form of religious life in which one is expected to conform to a pattern of belief and practice that is a fixed tradition. Not to conform is to lay oneself open to the accusation of being unspiritual or unsaved. This narrows and twists what the New Testament means by life.

A much less pious version of the same misrepresenta-tion takes place in some of our churches and is more diffi-cult to detect. The " life " that Jesus offers to men is iden-tified with what passes currently for the Christian life in the community. Children grow up taking for granted that the life of the good religious people around them is what they are offered in the gospel. This is the life which their seniors have attained as a consequence of their faith. It is a reasonable assumption, but a fatal one, for far too often what they have experienced is no more than a mediocre version of middle-class religiosity and morality. They re-ceive a healthy shock when the New Testament comes open to them and redefines the word " life " in its full depth and breadth. Perhaps the most paralyzing source of confusion and sterility in present-day Christianity is the mistaking of the safe, comfortable, decent order of exist-ence that we have fashioned for ourselves for the Christian venture into life.

The New Testament makes a stupendous claim — that the life for which men have hungered from the beginning of time was actually realized on earth in one person, a first-century Jew who lived thirty years of his life obscurely in the town of Nazareth in Palestine, but whose brief mission, whether one year or three, rudely terminated by a Roman cross, has made him the central decisive point for millions in the history of mankind. He founded no new religion, propounded no new philosophy, established no churches, wrote no books, and yet in the few months of his public ministry the life that was in him and came to expression in his words and actions became the source of new life for a little group of men and women and through them for an ever-increasing circle of persons. He possessed life in himself and was able to awaken the same life in others. The first step in the Christian faith must therefore be an encounter with him through the double witness of the New Testament and of the community of those who have genuinely received their life from him. We begin not with an argument, not with a complex of beliefs, not with a religious institution, but with a life that confronts us in a person, Jesus Christ, and offers itself to us to become our life. The dimensions of that life, whether it be his in its purity or ours in its brokenness and incompleteness, will be for us the dimensions of the Christian faith.

3

Religion

To most people Christianity is one among the many religions of the world, perhaps the highest and the truest, they hope, but with much in common with other religions. There was a time when Christians divided the whole of humanity really in two, with themselves in one compartment labeled " Saved " and all others indiscriminately in a great dark pit labeled " Lost." But the nineteenth century changed all that. Missionaries scattered themselves across the earth and in their endeavor to understand the peoples to whom they were sent, investigated their existing religions and brought back knowledge of them to the West. At the same time archaeologists deciphered the inscriptions of ancient Eastern cultures and brought to light among other things the religious beliefs and practices of ancient man. Scientific study of these religions, carried on parallel with the study of religious beliefs and practices in Old and New Testament times and in the whole history of the church, has produced drastic changes in our way of thinking. First, we find ourselves compelled to approach the non-Christian religions with respect. Even the most primitive religions are serious attempts by man to grapple with the mysteries of the world in which he finds himself, and the higher religions combine impressive insights into human problems with constructive contributions to the humanizing of society. Second, we observe many religious phenomena that are similar whether they occur in the Hebrew-Christian

tradition or in non-Christian religions, so that we are
forced to distinguish between elements that our tradition
has in common with other religions and elements that are
unique in Christianity. Third, every religion, including the
various forms the Christian religion has taken through the
centuries, is now seen to have a cultural context. It both
shapes and is shaped by the culture in which it exists. It
may lay claim to absolute truth and perfection in its formulations, but like the culture of which it is a part, it is a
relative human phenomenon and the inexorable changes
which history brings deal harshly with a religion that is
static in its structure.

The attitude engendered frequently by these developments is one of tolerance to all religions, combined with a
positive evaluation of Christianity as *our* religion, the religion most congenial to our Western civilization and one of
the essential foundations of order in our society. This attitude found fertile soil in America in which to grow, for a
strong tradition can be traced back to founders of the nation, such as Jefferson and Franklin, of approving religion
in general as an essential of the nation's life, but reducing
its basic definition to a few elements that can be found in
some form in almost all religions. There was nothing novel
in the sentiment expressed by a recent President that " religion is a necessity in our society, but it does not matter
too much what religion it is." One suspects that the amaz-
ingly high percentage of citizenry who belong to religious
institutions is more a product of this conviction than a
product of devotion to the particular tenets of the institutions, more an expression of support of religion as a bulwark of the good society than a commitment to a specific
faith. Let it be clear, however, that the developments that
have forced Christianity out of its former isolation and set
it in the context of multiple religions, at the same time
bringing to light the relativity of all expressions of religion,
did not need to issue in this attitude. In fact, it could do
so only when Christians were ignorant of what constitutes

the uniqueness of their own faith.

At the core of the Biblical tradition is a quarrel with religion which never ceases. The story of Moses and Aaron in the days of Israel's first beginnings is representative: Moses goes up the mountain to get instructions from God for the shaping of the nation's life, and while he is gone, the people, with Aaron as their priest, fashion an idol as the focal point of their worship and hold a religious celebration. To Moses this exuberant expression of popular religion and the life to which Israel is called as the peculiar people of God stand in irreconcilable opposition. The same tension appears again and again. The prophet Micaiah, with his warning of doom to the kings of Israel and Judah as they prepare for war against a neighboring state, stands alone in contrast to the four hundred official prophets of the national religion, who proclaim unanimously God's approval of the war; he could guard the future of his nation only by undermining the authority of a religion that put itself and its God unconditionally at the service of the national policy. For the prophet Amos the one indispensable evidence of faithfulness to God was that in the life of Israel even the poorest man should be dealt with justly and should have his opportunity, and he criticized the temple worship for letting its ritual of sacrifice and song become a substitute for obedience to God's will in the marketplace, the courts, and the common life. Jeremiah very nearly became a martyr when in the same spirit he attacked the Temple as the focal point of a national pride that was masquerading as true religion. Here then is the distinctive feature of Old Testament religion: it had within it a remarkable succession of prophets, and of people who stood with these prophets, who were constantly setting a question mark against the whole order of religion and life in Israel. They did not form a sect apart from the religious cult, but rather, by remaining in it contributed mightily to a reshaping of it and to the enrichment of its life. Yet in each new age they found themselves in critical tension with it.

The relation of Jesus to the established religion of his time shows a similar tension. Like Jeremiah he prophesied the destruction of the Temple of which his countrymen were so proud. His attack on the money changers in the Temple courts was an act of protest rather than an attempt at reform. The synagogue worship, at which he was a regular attender, was a much more impressive and effective religious institution than the Temple. The simplicity and meaningfulness of its prayers, its Scripture readings, and its sermons had made it for centuries a powerful educative force in Israel. The high level of religion and morality attained in it attracted many Gentiles to it in the Greco-Roman world. And yet we find Jesus sharply in tension also with the religion of the synagogue. It is to be seen most clearly in his conflict with Pharisees in whom synagogue religion came to its most earnest expression. They were diligent students of the Scriptures. They were firm believers in God. They were determined that the will of God as they knew it from the Scriptures and from their tradition should be obeyed in even the smallest details of life in Israel. But somehow in spite of their passionate devotion to God they had lost the living God. Their religion had become a mountainous obstacle between them and God. They had become more concerned to meet God's claim upon them by the performance of religious duties, some ritual, some moral, than by putting themselves at God's disposal to achieve his purposes in human life. Their religious zeal made them exclude from their worship and from community with themselves anyone who was unwilling to conform to their concept of religion, and they no longer understood God's care for all his creatures, Israelite or non-Israelite, religious or irreligious, and his will for man as man that he should live and not die.

Jesus did not condemn Pharisaism as a degenerate form of religion. We grasp the significance of Jesus' critique of it only when we appreciate how sincere the Pharisee was in his religion and in his concern for moral standards. The synagogue was morally and religiously superior to what is frequently to be found in our Christian churches. If the Pharisee, with his knowledge of Scripture, his scrupulous obedience to the commandments, his tithing on behalf of his church, his competence in prayer, and his passionate devotion to the cause of religion, were to appear in almost any Christian community today, people would be puzzled why Jesus was so severely critical of him. The question mark that Jesus set against Pharisaism he would set against all religion! Pharisaism in the New Testament highlights for us the danger of religion. Every form of religion has in it the danger of becoming not a highway to God but rather an obstacle between man and God blocking the highway on which God seeks to come to man. Jesus did not secede from Judaism and from the synagogue. He did not form a new religious institution which would forevermore preserve the one true religion in its purity. He did not encourage his followers to give up the existing forms of worship. Rather, as a loyal son of Israel and in conscious continuity with the prophetic tradition, he sought to restore Israel to its destiny as servant of God's purpose, not just for the sake of Israelites, but for the sake of all mankind that they should move forward to the fulfillment of their destiny. Religion came under his condemnation only insofar as it stood in the way of God's getting on with his work in the lives of men.

It is interesting and instructive to note this same tension with religious constructions in the first generation of the church's life. It is reasonably clear from Paul's letters and from evidence that is somewhat concealed in The Acts that as the Christian movement began to develop within the context of the Jewish community, some of the religious forms that it assumed were as uncongenial to Paul as Pharisaism had been to Jesus. Paul spent much of his life in conflict with a religion that bore the name " Christian," that considered itself the only true and authoritative form of Christianity and yet condemned his preaching as heretical.

Two things begin to be clear. It must always be questionable to speak of " the Christian religion," because at the very source of the Christian movement is a concern for man as man in the totality of his life that breaks through every religious formulation. By its very nature it reaches out to compass all men. Its aim is not to win them for a religion but to open to them the possibility of life, their own true life, and to make them agents of life instead of agents of death. The God of Jesus Christ is the living, life-giving God who hates death and conquers death on man's behalf. When Christianity becomes a religion intent only on making adherents, it is unfaithful to its own nature and to its God. It exists for this alone, that men, all men, may have life. Yet, and this is the second thing, as the divine concern for man's life becomes our concern, inevitably it comes to expression in ways that are religious and institutional. Even the most uninstitutional and anti-institutional expressions of concern find themselves compelled before long to become institutional in order to survive.

Against this background we can understand the current talk of " religionless Christianity," a phrase that originated with Dietrich Bonhoeffer. It contains in a new form the perennial protest of faith against a religion that claims to be Christian but no longer is aware that the primary concern of a Christian faith is with what is happening to men in the ordinary, everyday, so-called secular situations of life. The suggestion is that if men would forget about being religious for a time, they might learn to be Christian. But it is unrealistic to think that Christian faith could exist among men for any length of time in a religionless form, and when devotees of " religionless or secular Christianity " hold themselves aloof from everything that they consider religious in the church, they weaken their protest and divide the Christian community unnecessarily. Nevertheless, we must recognize that this protest against religion continues the central Biblical tradition and focuses our attention upon what is unique in a Biblical faith.

When Christians begin to think that respect for other religions compels them to abandon what seem to be extravagant and pretentious claims to universality in the New Testament faith, they have lost from sight this unique element which sets in question not only every human religious construction but also every established order of human society. It seems to them more modest to regard Christianity not as " a faith for every man " but rather as " the religion of Western man." They do not realize that they have sacrificed the very essence of their faith and have substituted for it a religion of which Jesus and the prophets would have been as critical as they were of the religions of their times. There *is* a " religion of Western man," congenial to the aims and values of our civilization, so interwoven with it that the two seem to many minds to be inseparable, but to call it Christian is to create confusion. It is a bulwark of the established order and gives to men a feeling of security, but insofar as we have made it our religion, the comforting and comfortable religion of an affluent society, we have abandoned the Christian faith. But let us be warned, a Christianity which in continuity with the Biblical tradition sustains a similar radical critique of religion and culture will not be likely to receive the kind of popular approval and support that is given to a " religion of Western man."

4

Gospel

WITHOUT FURTHER DELAY we must attempt to track down and define more clearly what we have called the unique element in Christianity. What is it that makes it burst through every religious formulation so that self-reformation is intrinsic to its nature? Where does it get the right to take the whole of mankind as its scope; or to put it more sharply, how does it come to have as its one legitimate aim the helping of every man alive to the fulfillment of his own true life? The source of these phenomena seems to lie in its *gospel*.

The power of self-reformation is certainly one of the most distinctive marks of Christianity, and the evidences of it are scattered all across the pages of its history. Reformation has often been represented as a return to the pure order of the earliest church. Protestant Reformers in the sixteenth century saw themselves as restoring the church to its original apostolic character. Lesser reformations since then have had the same aim. The Roman Church long maintained that it had preserved the original order intact. But each reformation, including the most recent one in Roman Catholicism, must be seen as not so much a restoration of any first-century order as a return to the original gospel, a fresh hearing of it that calls for a reshaping of the life of the church. New Testament research has disclosed that the early church, far from having achieved any perfect order, was itself involved just as we are in a struggle for the definition of its life and character. What gives it an authority for us is not any attainment of perfection but the clarity of its witness to the gospel.

The word " gospel," like its synonym " evangel " and the associated words " evangelical," " evangelist," and " evangelize," has been commandeered in recent years by a conservative type of Christianity, highly emotional and individualistic and focused intensively upon the gaining of immediate conversions, sometimes with a sophisticated technique for the encouragement of quick decisions. As a result the words have been narrowed in their meaning and have lost much of their New Testament breadth and depth. They need to be reclaimed for our use. The Old Testament background may help to build their Biblical context.

The prophet whom we call Second Isaiah (Isa., chs. 40 to 66) incites Jerusalem to become a " gospeler " or " evangelist " to the cities of Judah, to *bear the good news* to them that God has pardoned their sin and is opening to them a new future. His news was unbelievable to Israelites who had been scattered among the nations by the disasters with which the sixth century B.C. began. They could see nothing before them but national dissolution. Yet the prophet persisted in his claim that God had in store for Israel a future more glorious by far than anything that had been known in the past. The very mountains would be moved from their place to make possible the seemingly impossible. When we ask him the source of his confidence he tells us that he had only to open his ears to a word that had been sounding and resounding in the life of Israel from the beginning of its history. That which made Israel the peculiar people of God was a word from God that had been set in her heart and upon her lips, a word before which men might well tremble since it was the determining force in all history. In it was revealed the will of God for man's life. To stand against it was to court destruction, but to hear and obey was to be taken up into the unfolding of the purpose of God for humanity. This word had in it power to transform the life of a nation from the barrenness of a desert to the abundance of a fruitful land. The gospel of the prophet thus has as its content this word from God which sets before the nation a choice between life and death; it tells men how to live and not die. The word is addressed primarily to the community, and to the individual only in the context of the community, and obedience is defined not in terms of individual conduct but as a just and merciful order in the relations between rich and poor, ruler and ruled, priest and people, in the common life of the community. We should note also that although the prophet finds this word first of all in his nation's past, he hears it as a present word being spoken afresh each morning with relevance for the situation of the day. The word that he hears from the past opens his ears to hear the word that needs to be spoken in the present. He does not merely repeat some word from the past. Because what he hears is a matter of life or death for him and for his fellowmen he is compelled to speak, and because it promises life where there has been only death, it is " good news " or " gospel."

The New Testament choice of the word " gospel " to describe the preaching of both Jesus and the early church (and later for each of the collections of tradition concerning Jesus) undoubtedly is an echo of the prophet's usage. There are many other points of continuity between the last great Old Testament prophet and Jesus, and we could not better define Jesus' preaching and teaching than " good news from God of how to live and not die." Jesus had no technique for quick conversions. The number who responded to his preaching in his lifetime, however large the crowds may have been that at times gathered to hear him, seems to have been pitifully small, especially when compared with the results of mass evangelism in the past two centuries. He seems to have concentrated all his concern upon lodging his words in men's hearts and minds and to have counseled his disciples against expecting any great immediate response. The seed buried in men's lives would need time to grow and bear its harvest.

The earliest description of Jesus' gospel meets us in the summary of his first preaching: " The time is fulfilled; the kingdom of God is at hand; repent and believe the gospel " (Mark 1:15). That could be freely translated: " Now is the time when the life for which you and your fathers have longed has become possible; turn round and respond in faith to the good news." The heart of the gospel was the offer of life. The Fourth Gospel speaks of life or eternal life whereas the first three speak of the Kingdom of God or the Kingdom of Heaven. For Jesus' Jewish hearers the " Kingdom " had long been a familiar term to describe the goal of all God's purposes for human life, a world from which all injustice, evil, and suffering would be banished and in which all men would live at peace with one another. In announcing the hour of fulfillment, Jesus was not encouraging men to think that a golden age was about to dawn quite apart from anything they might do. Rather, he was countering the prevailing mood that the present order of the world with its frustration of life would continue until one day God would suddenly alter all things and establish his Kingdom. He was alerting men to expect God's new order to begin breaking in upon the old order now. Life was for them the broken, sickly, slavish thing it was, a literal death in life, because in spite of their religion they were blind to the living presence and power of God. They had their backs to God; they must turn and face him. Their ears were deaf to his voice; they must get for themselves new ears with which to hear. But what would they hear with these new ears? Not a series of religious propositions but the language of a new world within them and beyond them. Everything in the present world would be transformed in its meaning for them as they let it come open to the new world of God. They would be living at the very point where the Kingdom of God would be breaking in upon the present life of man. Here then was the beginning of the good news: Men do not need to be prisoners

of the evil forces in life; they do not need to live broken
and darkened lives; freedom and wholeness are possible —
in God!

We cannot understand Jesus' gospel without at the same
time understanding his diagnosis of man's dilemma. For
him the source of man's powerlessness, brokenness, futility,
and many of his physical sicknesses was in his self-centeredness, his focusing of his life in himself rather than beyond himself in God and neighbor. Man as man could not
be himself in isolation. The height and breadth of his own
life would be hidden from him until they were disclosed
to him in his relationships with God and with his fellowman. Moreover, the two relationships were inseparable.
He could not be open to God and closed against his fellowman or open to his fellowman and closed against God.
The essence of man's sin was an engrossment in self,
which did not necessarily take crude and vulgar forms but
could even determine the pattern of life of the most earnestly religious persons. In fact, the religious life, the good
life, could provide the most massive justification for man
in his self-centeredness. Like the rich young ruler, having
kept all the commandments from his youth up, the religious man was likely to find it quite unreasonable that God
should expect anything more of him, the unreason, of
course, being attributed not to God but to those who made
the claim on behalf of God. That which made religion
powerless to touch the real problems of men's lives was its
failure to grasp that there can be no halfway measures in
a relationship with God. It is all or nothing. Either he is
sovereign, that is, the center from which life is determined,
or he is absent. The gospel, therefore, is the offer to men
of a life and a world transformed by the presence of God
at its center. Sin is forgiven. Sicknesses are healed. Anxiety and fear which distort the self are overcome. A new
quality enters into life's relationships. But the Kingdom
cannot come or the new life begin without man's repentance, a break with the old world in which he is willing to

go only partway with God, a yielding of the place of rule in life to the present living God, a turning round to stand before God in the present moment.

The life of the Kingdom, of God's great new world, confronted men not just in Jesus' words but also in his person. It was not an ideal world held out to them in his teaching as a possibility, but rather, the actuality of his own existence. The perfectness of his obedience was the outward sign of the presence of the Kingdom in him. He proclaimed the hour of fulfillment because in him life *was* fulfilled. In recognition of this the early church did not just repeat his gospel but made his person the very center of its gospel. It heard God's word to man not just in his teachings but in him, and above all in the final events of his life with them in which he was most decisively revealed to them, his death and resurrection. It was no longer sufficient to say that like a prophet he spoke God's word to man; he was in himself, and in the whole unfolding of his life on earth, the final decisive word of God to man. In him the sin of man's self-centeredness was wholly overcome. In him our human life was reconciled with God. In him our world was invaded by God's new world, and in the conflict of the two, although he for the moment might seem to have been defeated, the stamp of death was set once and for all not upon him but upon the old world of man's self-centeredness. Men of faith saw the new world dawning.

Earlier I warned against the narrowing of meaning which the word " gospel " experiences at the hands of some modern evangelists. The content of the gospel becomes largely an appeal to men to repent and be converted rather than a setting forth of the word of God in its full, rich, Old and New Testament dimensions. The prophetic concern with the political, economic, and social dimensions of life disappears, and strong emphasis is placed instead upon what is going to be our fate in a world beyond this world. The Christian life takes on characteristics that are disturbingly similar to the strict religious legalism of the Pharisees.

Faith becomes tied to a Biblical literalism which absolu-
tizes everything that is Biblical as final truth and makes
men timid or downright frightened to translate Biblical
language, concepts, and symbols into terms that are meaningful in the twentieth century. But at one point criticism
must be silent. We can learn from the evangelists that the
preaching and the hearing of the gospel is a matter of life
or death, that none of us can ever hear it, even though it
be for the thousandth time, without being confronted with
a decision for or against God, and that means also for or
against our own true self.

5

God

MORE FOG GATHERS around the word " God " than around
any other word in the Christian vocabulary. We have been
using it thus far without defining it except insofar as it has
been defined by its context. It is impossible to say anything
significant about the Christian faith while leaving God out
of the picture. But the word is urgently in need of definition, both positively and negatively. It has become a rag-
bag of meanings, each of which aims at the truth and
misses it by a mile. What accentuates the fog is that many
of these meanings are given currency and the stamp of
validity by their presence in the preaching and teaching of
the church and are exempted from the criticism they de-
serve by receiving in men's minds something of the respect that belongs only to God himself.

Who has not heard a preacher wax poetic as he tells his
congregation to go out and, opening their souls to the beau-
ties of nature, drink in the very presence of God? Nature
does have a place in God's providence, but if men seek
God there, they are more likely to become pantheists than
Christians. Or who has not heard from his earliest years,
" What is to be will be," and formed a picture in his mind
of a God in some remote heaven who controls directly everything that happens on earth? It may generate a submis-
siveness under suffering, but it makes of God a tyrant and
a monster of cruelty. It is very definitely not what the
Scriptures mean by predestination; the God of Israel and

of Jesus Christ does not deal with men as though they
were puppets. Again, sentimentalism, building on Jesus'
practice of addressing God as Father and taking an indul-
gent and rather irresponsible father as its model, has come
up with a God from whom all severity of judgment has
been purged so that he is little more than a heavenly Santa
Claus. Another form of sentimentalism, a self-idealizing
which is widespread in a society where there is so much
concern for personality development, locates the " divine "
(there is a hesitation about saying " God ") in man's higher
nature, and every man is assured that he has a spark of the
divine within him. It usually passes unnoticed that a God
who is a spark is something less than a person. What is
being aimed at and missed is the Christian doctrine of the
indwelling of man by the Spirit of God, who is no spark
but God himself, and whose indwelling does not make man
divine but enables him as a mortal and sinful man to live
joyfully in the presence of God.

Among these mistaken substitutes for God we must list
also a form of idolatry that focuses upon Jesus. There are
Christians who, in honest rebellion against false concep-
tions of God and in despair of ever finding their way out
of the fog that surrounds his name, say to themselves, " I
need no other God than Jesus." They open their New Testaments and there stands Jesus before them as the very
model of perfection. All vagueness and confusion are gone
and faith has a clear and definite center on which to focus. However, the simplification is deceptive and issues in
a glorified, idealistic hero worship rather than in anything
remotely resembling the historic Christian faith. This is far
from what the early church meant by the divinity of Jesus,
" God in Christ."

Against this background we can perhaps understand the
measure of interest and approval that greeted the dramatic
announcement several years ago that " God is dead." Undoubtedly it gained a special piquancy and intellectual re-
spectability from the fact that it was made by professors of

theology or religion in reputable institutions of learning and received endorsement of a kind even from a bishop. But perhaps the most significant thing about it was that it encouraged a considerable number of people to admit that they were eager to get rid of God. God was to them a bore and a burden. And they were the more willing to have him dead when they were assured that there was no need to discard Jesus or the Christian way of life, that in fact an atheistic Christianity is only its most up-to-date form and the one that is most consonant with the maturity of the human race in the twentieth century.

But if maturity means facing the problems with which life confronts us in the light of men's experience with the problems in the past and with openness to the possibility of new answers, one might have expected of professors of theology and even of professors of religion somewhat more hesitancy in announcing that God was dead. It might have seemed to them a little presumptuous to assume that this dramatic and far-reaching negation at which they had arrived had never occurred to any of their predecessors. Humility might have suggested a less dramatic " God is dead for me." We could even agree with them if what they meant was that there are gods worshiped as the Christian God who are dead gods and who need to be exposed and buried. To believe in the God and Father of Jesus Christ is to disbelieve in all the false representations of God. One cannot say a meaningful yes to the true God without saying no to every substitute for God. In the Roman Empire the Christians were attacked and condemned as atheists because of their refusal to bow down to what the citizenry in general called " God." Dietrich Bonhoeffer in Germany in 1932 responded to the call of the Chancellor, von Papen, for a revival of the nation's faith in God by asserting that in relation to *this* God of the German nation he could only be an atheist. And even more recently there have been heads of state who have mouthed the name of God for their own purposes in a way to which the only

Christian response can be one of abhorrence. We have always to ask concerning a man's atheism whether, unrec-
ognized by him, it may be a rejection of false gods masquerading as Christian, in which case we as Christians have
to stand with him rather than against him. There are gods
who are a bore and a burden, gods who encourage men
in their selfishness and brutality, gods who crush men and
rob them of their freedom, gods who anchor men to some
order of the past and leave them helpless in the face of a
new and unexpected future. Like the Israelites before
them, Christians are constantly tempted to exchange their
God for one or other, or some combination of these gods,
but they cannot even know that they are tempted unless
they know with definiteness who their God is.

A Christian does not begin in midair to search for God,
analyzing the phenomena of life to see if he can find God
somewhere in the world beyond himself or in the world
within himself, or speculating about a power or person behind the universe. He begins with a history in which men
whose integrity he cannot question bear witness to what
God has been to them and to their people. They testify
that God " called " them to put themselves unconditionally
at his service. In generation after generation they respond
to this " call " which comes to them out of the unseen, and
their lives are shaped by it. In obedience to the voice of
God they become the protagonists of justice, truth, and
mercy in the relationships of men with one another in the
community, and they let themselves be judged and humbled before God in solidarity with their fellowmen. But
the word that judges them contains within it a promise of
what life can be if lived in openness to God and to the future that God intends for man. We do not start " from
scratch " to interrogate the universe concerning God. We
start in confrontation with this testimony. We stand together with an Amos or a Jeremiah, a Paul or a John, to
see if we can hear what once they heard. Was the word
that came to them the word of truth not only for them but

also for us? We do not seek God in vacancy but in a concrete word in human language that claims to be a word from him to us.

It is blindness on our part, however, to think that the initiative in the seeking is with us. According to the Biblical testimony, God long ago took the initiative and came in search of man. When we penetrate to the earliest beginnings of Israel's distinctive life, the only explanation of how this strange nation came to be is that God " called " them to put themselves at his service, and in a personal covenant relationship with him to have incorporated in them the life that is the only true life of man. The history of Israel is a history of obedience in the midst of disobedience. Obedience in the covenant relation, because it was a free response in love to the love that had called them out of slavery and given them a future, made Israelites not slavish but free men, free as no other men were free. God alone was their king in a way that made them the enemies of every human tyranny. Disobedience, unfaithfulness to the covenant, allegiance to other gods, however, were in almost every generation more popular than faithfulness and eventually undermined the nation's existence. But no unfaithfulness could undermine or dim the testimony of the faithful in Israel to what God was to them. They sang it in their psalms. The prophets, grasped by it, took their lives in their hands to withstand the national corruption and mark out the road on which alone there was promise of a future. The historians wrote a unique kind of history, depicting not just the doings of men but the interaction of God and man within the covenant relation across the centuries.

The New Testament takes up anew the record of this servant people of God — but with a difference. The core of the Old Testament was a call, a word, a command, that was heard from the Beyond. God was ever coming to his people in his word, and they lived in expectation of fresh comings. The core of the New Testament is the same call, the same word, the same command, but present now in the midst of men in a person, so that the center out of which the church was born was a servant of the word, in whom servant and word were so completely one that God's presence in his word was now God's presence in a person, an incarnation, Immanuel, which is Hebrew for " God with us." " The word was life and the life was the light of men." This word in Jesus, in his life and most powerfully of all in his death, called men into its service, and the community of the " called " eventually became the Christian church. Again the initiative was from beyond man. Men did not search for God, find him in a new way, and institute a new religion. God in his word in the Galilean Jesus initiated a new era in human history. He came seeking men for his service and in his call to them wrenched them out of the old order of their life and sent them venturing into an uncharted future.

But in sending them on their mission, he came to them in yet one more new way. He did not let his presence with man in human flesh terminate with the death of Jesus. His word and action in Jesus did not become something merely to be remembered by Christians. The life that had broken in upon the world in Jesus, the very life of God incarnate in man, was renewed in those who, remembering the word that they had heard in him, found themselves possessed and indwelt by the same Spirit of God whose presence and power in him had been the source of his unique life and mission. The Christian's life was not just a following of the way that had been marked out by Jesus; it was a participation with Jesus in the life and mission of the new era that had been initiated in him. Paul could describe the intimacy of the relation only by saying that Jesus Christ lived afresh in him. By that he was describing not so much some inner experience or an imitation of Jesus' life as the action of the same Spirit of God that empowered Jesus for his mission among men, empowering and directing Paul and his fellow Christians as they carried the same mission to the ends of the earth.

The Christian content of the word " God " is marked out for us by that history, so that when we say " God " as Christians, we have to say three words or we have stopped short of Christian truth. The doctrine of the Trinity, which has had many harsh things said about it in recent years, has to be understood as the church's attempt to describe in a brief formula how it came to know God and how alone a Christian can rightly know God. He is the God who from the beginning has been calling man into a covenant relation with himself in which alone life in this world makes sense and has a future. When his call from beyond our world was insufficient, he came to us in a person of our own flesh and blood and in him knocked on the door of our human life. He came in search of us in Jesus Christ, and where men let themselves be found, he took possession of their very selves, indwelt them with his Spirit, and through them extended his search for man. The Trinity describes God's invasion of our world, and the question for us is how we shall respond to this Invader. Faith in him is surrender to his invasion, openness to the life he brings, readiness to let the life that comes to us from him go on through us to others.

6

Resurrection

IN MUCH OF OUR USAGE, " Jesus " and " Christ " have become simply two names for the same person which may be used separately or together. The story of Jesus and Simon Peter at Caesarea Philippi warns us that this has not always been so. For Simon to call Jesus " Christ " was a decisive moment in his discipleship. He had penetrated past the surface, not all the way, but at least far enough to touch the secret of Jesus' being. It was something that he could not know through any of the ordinary ways of knowing. The Father in heaven had revealed it to him, Jesus told him. In keeping with this was Jesus' constant unwillingness to have men speak of him as " the Christ." For most Jews of his day the Christ was a mysterious, semidivine, all-powerful conqueror who would come in the name of God to set Israel free from foreign domination and to establish on earth an era of justice and peace in which Israel as the chosen nation of God would rule for him. More than one Jew of Jesus' day, giving himself out as " the Christ," or being so regarded by his followers, had sponsored a futile rebellion. We have only to remind ourselves that Jesus was crucified by the Romans on suspicion of being one such troublesome " Christ " to realize how dangerous and misleading it was to have this term applied publicly to him. Not until he had died was it possible for him to be called " the Christ " without raising false expectations.

Some New Testament scholars insist that Jesus had no thought of himself as " the Christ," and it is true that it was not in his lifetime but in the early Jewish Christian church that he was freely given this name. This can suggest that, although the early church recognized the fulfillment in him of the Old Testament's outreach toward a new era and the initiation of a new covenant relation between God and man, Jesus himself was wholly unaware of his relation to that prophetic hope and promise. There can be no doubt that he repudiated the popular conception of " Christ " or " Messiah " (which is the Hebrew term). There is evidence, however, not only in the account of his experience at baptism but at many other points, that he saw the prophetic hope, so strong and clear in Second Isaiah, for a messianic servant of the word who would be willing even to die in faithfulness to his task, being somehow fulfilled in him — and through him in those whom he would bind to him in the same service. Therefore, although Jesus rejected one form of Messiahship, another concept, servanthood, rooted at a deeper level in the prophetic faith, was at the very core of his understanding of his destiny. His consciousness of Sonship, expressed in his use of the child's term " Abba " in addressing God as his Father in prayer, points in the same direction. To be a son of God was to be like God. This was what man was created to be, and the loss of sonship was the loss of his destiny. The recovery of sonship was the restoration of man to his true nature and to his true place in the creation. It would be strange to deny to Jesus any consciousness of the uniqueness of this sonship when the sharing of it with others was the purpose of his mission. " Christ of God," " Son of God," these were Old Testament concepts that were transmuted and came forth with new meaning in Jesus' understanding of himself. They express the secret both of his being and of his mission, but they were hidden in him to be revealed only to faith, for he would have created only misconceptions if he had tried to speak directly of such mysteries. And yet the word " Christ " is bandied about by us as though anyone with the slightest acquaintance with Christianity should know what it means. Its meaning was hidden in Jesus' lifetime and it is hidden still today, however often we may have used the word, unless the secret of Jesus' being and of his mission have been revealed to us in it.

The resurrection of Jesus from the dead had decisive significance for the birth of the Christian church because it was for the disciples, and later for Paul, the disclosing of that secret, the unveiling of God's presence, action, and mission in the person of Jesus. What had been hidden from them in his lifetime was revealed to them in his death and resurrection. His death stripped them of all false expectations concerning the Messiah, and his resurrection opened their eyes to what Jesus had been about from his first coming among them. It enabled them to see him as the climactic fulfillment of the purpose of God which bound all their past history together. Even his death had been foreshadowed in the Old Testament as necessary if God's Kingdom was to have its victory over the stubborn disobedience of men.

The resurrection of Jesus is to many people the most incredible claim of the Christian faith. It is not the kind of thing that happens in our world. In fact, if someone came to them and asserted that a person of their acquaintance who died three days previously and was buried had appeared to him as though alive, they would be inclined to doubt their informer's sanity. What complicates matters further is that in some quarters the resurrection of Jesus is understood as a resuscitation of a dead man, so that the ascension of Jesus to the right hand of God becomes the movement of a physical body upward into the skies until it arrives at a place " up there " called heaven. Moreover, this version is able to claim considerable support from stories in the New Testament of the risen Jesus doing such things as eating, though other stories point to the unsubstantial nature of the resurrection body. But however great the difficulties, nothing can conceal how central and all-important the resurrection of Jesus was for the first Christians. It may be explained or interpreted in various ways — as hysterical visions of a trusted leader, as inner experiences in which faith in Jesus as their Messiah came to birth in the disciples, or as actual events in which Jesus continued to reveal himself to his disciples beyond his death — but there is clear historical evidence that the Christian church owed its very being to the resurrection of Jesus. Paul could say that if Jesus was not risen from the dead, then all the hopes that Christians placed in him were without foundation. Paul's own Christian life had begun when he was confronted by the risen Lord as the ultimate revelation of the truth and purpose of God, but in this he counted himself at one with the earliest disciples of Jesus.

Paul's vision of Jesus on the Damascus road is perhaps the best starting point for a discussion of the resurrection. In his letter to the Galatians, Paul describes it as, " When it pleased God to reveal his Son in me." " Reveal " here does not have the meaning of disclosing information. Paul already, as a persecutor of Christians, must have had an abundance of information about Jesus. He would not have concluded that the Christian movement was dangerous to the established order of religion and should be exterminated without having investigated the teachings and actions of Jesus. He was familiar also with the claim that the crucified Jesus had risen from the dead and was for his followers none other than the Messiah of Israel. Paul undoubtedly knew much about Jesus and had no liking for what he knew. The reality of Jesus and of the new age for man that had dawned in him was hidden from Paul. Therefore the resurrection experience for him was a revealing of what had been hidden, not as further information or as divine truths, but as a life that was being offered to him in the person of Jesus and that became a new existence for him as a man when he responded in faith. Hence-

forward his life was a life that he could describe as either
" in Christ " or " Christ in me." The resurrection was for
him the initiation of a new age, a new world, in which,
through God's awesome presence in Jesus, a new humanity
was possible for every man, a humanity made new by its
reconciliation with God.

It is a mistake to think of Jesus' resurrection as " proving " to the disciples and to Paul that he was the Messiah.
Revealing that he was the Messiah is something other than
" proving." " Proving " suggests too much a purely intellectual operation. Revelation, as with Paul, means a confrontation with God, in which one's whole being is laid
open to God. The blind see and the deaf hear. It may help
us if we set alongside this resurrection experience some
other accounts of revelation in the Scriptures. There is
Isaiah's own account of his call to be a prophet (Isa.,
ch. 6). It was as though God were there before him like a
great monarch sitting upon a throne and with his robes
sweeping down to fill the temple. The sovereignty of God
over the whole earth, the holiness of God demanding righteousness of all who would stand before him, the urgency
of God's purpose in history and his lack of anyone to speak
for him, the readiness of God to cleanse a man of his sin
with forgiveness and so make him ready for his service —
all this dawned upon the soul of Isaiah in that moment,
but not as something apart from himself. It tore away all
his illusions about himself, stripped him naked before God,
and made him covet one thing alone in life: to be taken
into the service of God and counted worthy of fellowship
with him. Revelation for Isaiah was a life-transforming in-
breaking of God upon him.

An even closer parallel to Paul's experience is that of
Moses, which led to the birth of Israel as the people of
God (Ex., ch. 3). Moses, like Paul, saw only a fiery light
and heard only a voice addressing him out of the fiery
light, but he knew that he was standing before God and

that God was claiming him, and his people with him, for his service.

The disciples had heard the call of God in Jesus' preaching, and they had responded by joining him in his mission. But they were not fully aware of what was happening in him, not just for them, but for all humanity. His endeavor was to take them into the very life with God that was his own. But the time was short and the resistance of the human self was strong. How strong it could be is dramatized for us in the histories of Peter and of Judas. Men, still centered in self and not in God, and blinded, as we all are, by their old ways of seeing things, had not the eyes to see deeply enough into Jesus to recognize what God was doing in him. His death, however, shattered their self-centeredness and humbled them. We need only think of Peter who learned in sorrow how far he was from sharing his Master's faith. Humbled and broken, the disciples were given new eyes with which to see. The resurrection was the revelation to them of God's continuing presence and action in Jesus. Once and for all they knew him as he was, God's word in human flesh, God's creation of a new humanity, the dawn of a new age in human history. The resurrection was nothing less than Jesus fulfilling the purpose of his mission, coming to his disciples in such a way that his coming was the coming of God himself to them and his presence with them a sharing with them of his own life in God. That he who had died should be able to impart such life to them and to offer it through them to all men was witness that the life they had from him was beyond the reach of death, life eternal and life triumphant.

7

Faith

"FAITH" SHARES ABOUT EQUALLY with "God" in having a confusing multiplicity of meanings placed upon it. What was perhaps the worst sermon I have ever heard defined it in rapid succession as (*a*) the confidence which enables us to drink water even though we know it has germs in it, (*b*) the divine spark hidden in every human soul, (*c*) the something that Peter had that enabled him to walk on water, and (*d*) trust in Jesus for everything. How is the intelligent hearer to respond when after listening to such an exposition, he is exhorted or invited to "have faith"? He is being sent in four different directions at once, and it is not surprising if, in exasperation, he goes in a fifth direction of his own choosing.

To complicate matters, there is a wide range of meaning that is sanctioned by the dictionary. These are meanings that have established themselves by common usage. A list of them (from *The American College Dictionary*) is instructive: "(1) confidence or trust in a person or thing, (2) belief which is not based on proof, (3) belief in the doctrines or teachings of religion, (4) the doctrines which are or should be believed, (5) a system of religious belief: *the Christian faith, the Jewish faith,* (6) the obligation of loyalty or fidelity (to a person, promise, engagement, etc.): *to keep or break faith with,* (7) the observance of this obligation: *to act in good or bad faith,* (8) Theologically: that trust in God and in his promises as made through

Christ by which man is justified or saved." But even the
dictionary recognizes that there is one meaning distinctly
different from all the common meanings and sets it apart
from the others as " theological." It would be an achieve-
ment if the preaching and teaching of the church were always as discriminating as the dictionary.

Three of the dictionary definitions require our attention
because they are so frequently taken to be definitions of
Christian faith, and the degree of truth in them leads men
into a wilderness of error. It is true that faith is a confidence, but confidence, as we shall see, of a very special
kind and not to be confused with either self-confidence or
the mutual confidence that makes social relations possible
or the confidence in life that enables one to go on living in
spite of the uncertainties that are always there, though it
most certainly has a bearing on all three of these forms of
confidence. A really Christian faith destroys all a man's
confidence in himself and yet at the same time enables him
to accept his very self with all its limitations, and the situation in which he finds himself, with the assurance that
from here and only from here does life begin for him. No
one can live as confidently as the Christian who has lost all
confidence in himself. His confidence has deeper roots beyond himself.

The same paradox operates in social relations. The mutual confidence on which they are based may be no deeper
than congeniality of temperament, similarity of interests,
and agreement of viewpoint. Where this is true a really
Christian faith may be disruptive of social relations, de-
veloping in the believer interests and convictions which
make him follow a course contrary to that of his neighbors
and which make them begin to distrust his judgment. Yet
the same faith lays a much deeper foundation for community, breaking through the superficial, deceptive, and
frequently stagnant mutuality which cannot bear the strain
of honest differences to establish relations in which there
are infinite possibilities of growth through the willingness

of members of the community to hear the truth from one another and not just echoes of their own minds.

The definition of faith as " belief which is not based on proof " has in it also a vestige of truth that makes it deceptive. It is true that no one can prove satisfactorily the existence of God. All the traditional arguments are effective only in reinforcing the assurance of those who already believe in God. Rarely are they convincing to the most open-minded agnostic or atheist. It is significant that among all the witnesses to the reality of God who meet us in the Scriptures, not one ever attempts in any way to prove that God exists. There is something intrinsic to their way of knowing God which makes proofs irrelevant. So also with the Christian belief in the divinity of Jesus. Through the centuries there have been misguided attempts by Christians to prove its truth in various ways, but all they have ever achieved is a concealment or perversion of its truth.

To go on from this, as men have done, to divide all knowledge into two compartments — that which is known by rational proof and that which is known by faith — is to invite disaster. Faith then tends to become a religious explanation of the phenomena of life, which survives only as long as science is unable to provide us with an explanation based on evidence. Three hundred years ago Christian theologians who should have known better fought Galileo's new explanation of the structure of the universe because it contradicted the earth-centered universe in which they believed. Christians have been slow to learn, and some unfortunately have still not learned, that faith is not a supernatural way of knowing facts about the world and man and history. Nor is faith a less certain way of knowing than reason. To faith is given a knowledge of God, of his purpose in the world, and of the meaning of man's life that has certainty of a kind *beyond* any of the tentative conclusions of science, a confirmation that is inseparable from the meaning which the believer finds in the events of life itself. Faith makes sense of life, which is something more than proof.

The third misconception that gets its wide currency from the element of truth in it is that faith consists in the acceptance of certain doctrines that have been formulated by the church. The Roman Church has its dogmas which must be believed if one is to be saved. Protestantism, also, has across the centuries had various versions of the same thing, a set of doctrines being forced upon men's minds as essential for both their temporal and their eternal good. *Both* Catholics and Protestants have at times in the past used not only social and psychological pressures but also the threat of physical punishments and even death itself to persuade men to accept the " right " doctrines. One of the positive achievements of nineteenth-century liberalism was to free men from this monstrous perversion of faith, but in doing so, it frequently went to the opposite extreme and lost from sight the importance of doctrinal formulations of the past for the definition of faith. In rebellion against doctrinal tyranny, Christians opted for a vaguely defined Christianity which has proved defenseless against the aggressive non-Christian faiths of the modern age that have been offering themselves as substitutes for Christian faith or even as an up-to-date version of the faith itself. Doctrines are the product of the church's attempt to spell out in detail the length and breadth, the height and depth, of its faith. From the very beginning it has been forced to do this, first by the inborn necessity of human beings to understand the faith to which they have committed themselves, to see with clarity what it requires of them, and to give an account of it to their fellowmen, and then in order to defend its truth against the misconceptions and perversions to which it has ever been subject. But such doctrinal statements are to be recognized as guides for Christians in their understanding of their own faith and not paper tyrants compelling submission. And faith itself dare not ever be identified with the acceptance of doctrines. It has been demonstrated only too often that men who are scrupulous about correctness of doctrine can lack many of the marks of a really Christian faith.

The striking thing about Jesus' use of the word " faith " is that it seems to be almost a synonym for " God." To persons who have been healed or set on a new road in life by God's forgiveness he says, " Your faith has saved you." Would it not have been truer and less open to misunderstanding if he had said, " *God* has saved you "? Or again, in his words to the disciples, " If you had faith as a grain of mustard seed, you would say to the mountains, Be removed," the very power of God seems to reside in the faith of men! Where faith is present, the power of God is present. Jesus here makes claims for faith that we would be reluctant to make! He attributes to the faith of a man what seems to us to belong to God alone! That is because we make a separation between God and man, an intrinsic separation, an unbridgeable gulf, which he could not make. Faith for us is at best a believing in the God, a relationship with the God, who stands on the other side of the gulf. But for Jesus that gulf of alienation is the tragically paralyzing and disrupting error of man's existence. For him God and man belong together with no gulf between, no alienation. God with man and man with God is the consummation of life. He knew that consummation in himself as wholeness, health, fulfillment, the Kingdom of God on earth, the only existence worthy to be called life, and his mission was to share it with others. Forgiving sin was not the brushing away of surface defects in men but the bridging of the gulf, the overcoming of the alienation, between man and God. Faith was an unconditional openness to God so that God was no longer distant or absent, but present. And the presence of God with man was the presence of God's power and love in man. The futility of religion lay in its acceptance of the gulf between God and man so that it could be at best the worship of a distant God, purporting to establish good relations with him — at a distance — and in doing so, concealing the depth of the gulf that still separated man from God.

We have not yet considered why Jesus found faith such a rarity among men or how faith comes to be. We must leave that for a later chapter.

In the next chapter we shall look more closely at the gulf of alienation. Here we must try to grasp what our definition of faith says to us about our life as human beings. We have a strong tendency to think of our existence as something that we have primarily in ourselves and that is then enriched or transformed by the relationships that we have with other persons. The relationships we consider to be at our disposal. We can withdraw from any or all of them, if we see fit, and have our existence only in our own self. Our relationship with God we include with the others. The choice is ours whether we are to have to do with him or not. But this whole way of thinking is unrealistic, untrue to the facts of life. From our first breath we have our existence only in personal relationships. We grow only in interaction with others. At every stage of life we are what we are because of what others past and present have been to us. We have our existence in a network of human relationships, and a disruption of those relations is a disruption of our existence. Experiments in the isolation of individuals in recent years have shown that a complete isolation from human contact very quickly brings an impoverishment of consciousness and a loss of self-identity. The Christian faith holds that what is true of our relations with persons past and present is true also of our relation with God. It is no elective but belongs inescapably to our existence. We have no possibility of being ourselves in isolation from God. We can disrupt the relationship, but we cannot destroy it. Our life comes to us from beyond ourselves, and our health is the health of the relationships in which we exist. Faith, then, is an openness to the presence and power of God, an openness to the purpose of God that men should live and not die, and therefore an openness and readiness to be used in the unfolding of that purpose for the whole of humanity. The power of faith, as we learn from the cross of Jesus, is a hidden power, very different from what we usually conceive of as power, but the only effective power in overcoming the forces that rob man of his true existence and in freeing men for the life for which they were created.

8

Sin

A GROUP OF MEN AND WOMEN arranged to meet with a theologian to hear what he would answer to questions about the Christian faith that had been troubling them. One of their number, a well-educated man who occupied a position of considerable responsibility, had not been present at the first meeting, so was given priority at the second. The theologian anticipated a question of some complexity, but what he heard was this: " What is sin? I have asked the question of five ministers and have never heard a satisfactory answer yet." Set alongside that the outburst of a woman who was engaged in Christian work and a regular participant in the worship of her church: " I get sick and tired of hearing so much talk about sin and of being told over and over that I am a sinner." The two incidents together reflect what is perhaps a very general response to the word " sin." It is something rather terrible and disgraceful of which people en masse feel that they are being accused by the Christian church, but no one ever makes sufficiently clear what this something is for it to strike home to the consciences of the hearers. They feel themselves victims of an accusation that applies to someone other than themselves.

It is curious but interesting that Harry Overstreet, in his *The Mature Mind,* regards the very idea of sin as inconsistent with the innate dignity of man and tries to free Jesus of the stigma of ever having harbored such an idea by alleging that it was first introduced into Christianity by Augustine. In defiance of the historical evidence, he makes Jesus over in the image of an intelligent Greek for whom there was no such thing as sin but only error. It is much less troublesome and humiliating to say " All men err " than to say " All men sin." But sin is not to be so easily dismissed from the Christian alphabet.

First, we must take account of the difference between Jesus and his religious contemporaries on the subject of sin. Their attitude in a modernized form frequently passes as Christian, and Jesus' attitude is lost from sight. Sin for them was any infraction of the laws of God, which consisted not just of the Ten Commandments but of all the ritual and moral laws of the Old Testament plus hundreds of unwritten laws that had been formulated across the years to make explicit what God required of man in the conduct of his life. A righteous man was one who kept the law scrupulously, a sinner one who broke the law or was careless in its observance. It was forbidden that a righteous man should have anything to do with sinners. The community of the righteous had to be kept pure. Therefore, in each Jewish town or village there was a sharp line of separation between the righteous and the sinners. Only the righteous were welcome in the worship of the synagogue.

This whole order was obnoxious to Jesus. It lent itself so easily to hypocrisy. Jesus by birth and upbringing belonged to the righteous half of the community and was a regular worshiper in the synagogue. But he had eyes to see how false the situation was. Here was one man, confident of his righteousness because of his constant care to obey all the ritual laws but neglecting the care of his own parents. Here was another, congratulating himself on his generosity to the poor, his honesty, his purity, his fasting, and his tithing, and looking down as though from a great height upon all " sinners." It was so easy to be respectably righteous and yet at some essential points utterly godless. At the same time it was possible to be branded a sinner and excluded from the worship of the synagogue, not because of any moral offense, but through a refusal to conform to the static pattern of the dominant religious community. Tax gatherers were automatically excluded, not as is sometimes alleged because they were invariably dishonest, but because their service to the Roman authorities was taken to be an act of treachery against their own people.

Jesus rejected categorically the division of the community into righteous and sinners. We should note that that division had been able to claim considerable validation from the Old Testament, particularly from The Psalms, but also from the Prophets, where the righteous and the unrighteous seem to stand sharply over against each other. But so to divide them was to ignore those passages in the Old Testament which set a question mark against all human righteousness. Jesus stood in line with this deeper and more fundamental strain in the Old Testament when he condemned the distinction between righteous and sinners as false and regarded it as a cruel, destructive device in the service of religious pride. In his eyes no man had the right to count himself good or righteous. He refused to let himself be called " good " by a man who was already a prisoner of his own self-righteousness. " Only God is good! " On another occasion he put the whole of mankind into a little parable in which the righteous are represented by a man who owes only a small debt to God and the sinners by one who owes God a very great debt (Luke 7:41-42). Both, that is, all, are hopelessly in debt to God and have nothing with which to discharge the debt. All are dependent equally on his forgiveness. That is the predicament of humanity. But that also is the homely and humiliating truth to which man closes his eyes. The truth is concealed, and the community is falsely split apart by the supposition of some that a reasonable measure of obedience to the laws of God and man will be accepted by God as a full discharge of their debt to him. Therefore Jesus' most cutting attack was not against the grievousness of sinners but against ev-

ery form of self-righteousness by which men deluded themselves as to where they stood with God.

Jesus offended the religious community of his time very
deeply by his refusal to recognize its distinction between
righteous and sinners. This was undoubtedly one of the
factors that led to his being regarded as a threat to the established order. He refused to confine his activities to the
religious sector of the community and was found ever more
frequently in the homes of tax collectors and others who
were branded as sinners. The fact that he ate with them
was an offense against the ritual law. When he was criticized, he defended himself with a touch of humor by asking whom he should be calling to repentance except sinners
and to whom he as a physician should be going except to
sick men. His words reflect his experience with the self-
styled " righteous." They had no ears for a word that would
have humbled them before God and thereby would have
opened for them a door to a new world. They were oblivi-
ous of the sickness of their own selves, their imprisonment
in a grossly inadequate structure of life, so that the healing
mission of Jesus was of no real interest to them.

It is significant that in this confrontation Jesus described
sin as sickness and himself as a physician sent to cure this
sickness. This should be basic for all Christian thinking
concerning sin. The sickness has its classic portrayal in Jesus' parable of the prodigal, with which he answered his
critics. The story begins with a father and two sons. Again,
as in the other parable, the two stand as representatives of
the " sinners " and the " righteous," but before the parable
is ended we realize that in actuality they represent two
forms of alienation from God. The one son, driven by the
urge to be his own master and to have his life in independence of his father, sets a great distance between himself
and his home; the other, more disciplined, less rebellious,
remains close to home and serves his father through the
years, and yet for all his closeness and his service has no
understanding of his father's heart and mind. Both are ob-

jects of the father's love, but both are separated from him by a great gulf. That is their sickness. That is the sickness of humanity. And it is far more difficult for the " righteous " son to be aware of his sickness than for the " sinner."

Now we have an illustration of how subtly truth can become falsehood. We have heard from Jesus that sin is sickness. It is so easy, however, for us to hear that as though he were saying, " Sin is *only* a sickness," and to conclude that no one should feel more responsible or guilty about it than he does about a physical sickness. Sin is then hardly as serious a matter as error. But Jesus cannot be accused of making light of sin. He stands directly in line with the whole prophetic tradition in the Old Testament for which sin is the great blind destructive force in human life. Sin is sickness, but a sickness unto death! To sin is to become a prisoner of the forces in ourselves and in society that pull men down and rob them of their life.

If sin is a sickness of man, then he is not by nature a sinner. Rather, sin is a corruption of his nature. This must be made very plain because it is often obscured, and the impression is created that Christianity degrades men in general as sinners and exalts only those who as Christians have been freed from sin, in short that it has a low view of humanity. The contrary is true. We have already seen that for Jesus, man is truly man only when he is at one with God, not in some kind of mystic absorption that lifts him out of the world, but in an unconditional openness to God that lays him open also to his fellowman and to life. The self cannot find itself within itself because it is impossible to be a human self except in a responsive and responsible relationship with God and with one's fellows. Sin destroys the self by disrupting the relationships on both levels.

That was not by any means a new understanding of man or of sin initiated by Jesus. It is embodied graphically in the two stories of Creation. Man was made in the image of God. It is his nature and his destiny to reflect in his human

existence the very nature of God. Psalm 8, a song of Creation, says that he was made " a little lower than God." To
be truly man he must be like God, with the faithfulness,
mercy, justice, truth, and holiness of God mirrored in his
existence with his fellowmen. This is the essence of humanity, but its source is not in man but beyond man in
God. It becomes a human possibility only when man's life
is lived in an openness to God that makes him open also in
his relationships with men. The constant plea of all the
prophets was for humanity and against every form of inhumanity, for justice and mercy in the order of society. Always for them the source of inhumanity in Israel was a
rupture of the personal covenant relation of the nation with
God, and a recovery of humanity was inseparable from a
return to God. Wholeness of life for society, as for the individual, was the product of a oneness with God in personal relation that had its closest analogy in the oneness of
man and wife.

But there was in man an enemy of his health and wholeness. Genesis, ch. 3, dramatizes it as a voice man hears
urging him to assert his independence of God and see what
he can make of life on his own, which is very similar to
the first bold steps of the prodigal in Jesus' parable. Then
man, having made himself the center of his world, quickly
finds himself the victim of fear and rivalry in his relations
with those about him. Sin thus begins to define itself as a
self-centeredness and self-assertion in which man proceeds
to construct for himself the kind of world that he prefers,
with little thought either of God or of his fellowmen. And
the more intent he is upon his self-realization, the more
tightly the doors become closed against God and man. The
relationships in which alone he can ever be himself wither
and die.

Only in the New Testament, however, does sin show itself fully as the enemy of life and of God. We constantly
assume that where there are moral earnestness and religious concern sin is at least minimized. But in the story of

Jesus' life and death, moral earnestness and religious concern are men's strongest defense against the God who meets
them and claims them in the words and actions of this man
and the source of their good conscience in sending him to
his death. We know the infinite deceptiveness of sin only
when the cross has done its work in us, has torn from us
our illusions about ourselves and exposed in us that stubborn core of resistance that, even when we think ourselves
most faithful, still builds barriers against God and man.
Nothing is more difficult for a good, religious, faithful
church member to grasp than that his goodness and religiousness, when he uses them to justify himself before
God, become the servants of his sin, blinding him both to
the truth concerning himself and to the future God has in
store for him.

9

Reconciliation

WHEN PAUL WISHED to sum up the significance of Jesus Christ for the whole of mankind, he wrote, " God was in Christ reconciling the world to himself," and then he brought all Christians for all time into the picture when he added, " and he has committed to us the ministry of reconciliation." It must at first seem incredible that what happened in a brief span of time in the life of a young Jew in a tiny Middle Eastern country should be regarded as having once and for all overcome the alienation that from the beginning of history has been poisoning human existence. Yet that is the claim not of Paul alone but of all the varied witnesses in the New Testament, each of them expressing it in his own way. To the early Christians it was nothing less than the dawn of a new age, the age of fulfillment, in the life of mankind.

But when we turn to the actual ministry of Jesus, what we see is an intensive mission to the neglected outsiders among Jesus' fellow countrymen in Palestine. He undertook no mission to the world. Only in very exceptional instances did he make contact with any of the non-Jews who were all about him in Palestine. And even within his Jewish world he limited the scope of his mission mainly to those Jews who belonged in the nonreligious section of the community. " I am not sent but to the lost sheep of the house of Israel." This does not mean that he avoided contact with religious Jews. We find him being entertained in their homes, and the synagogue was one of the places where he taught. But among them he met little understanding or acceptance for his gospel in comparison with the welcome that he received among the outsiders.

This difference in Jesus' reception among the religious and among the outsiders was directly due to the nature of his mission. He was a physician concerned with the cure of sin. To him all men were sick with the same disease, a brokenness in their very self, an inability to be themselves because of a rupture in their relationship with God, which worked itself out not only in physical and spiritual consequences in the individual but also in a social paralysis. His remedy for the sickness was the forgiveness of God. This was his good news: Human existence does not need to remain broken, poisoned, paralyzed; personal relationships, either of man with his fellowman or of man with God, which have been ruptured by offenses, can be made whole again; sin is not intrinsic to the nature of man and as such to be accepted as the normal condition of his life, but can be cleansed and conquered by the forgiveness of God. Jesus' cold reception among the religious was their honest response to his message. They did not consider themselves in need of such a physician. The problem of sin was not one that troubled them. But among the outsiders Jesus found a willingness to acknowledge that life was a problem for them and to listen when he spoke of what could be done about it. Among them he could get on with his mission.

How Jesus did his work as a physician is what interests us. His remedy for man's sin was the forgiveness of God. However, he did not apply the remedy by merely talking to men about forgiveness. He forgave them. Before they heard anything about forgiveness in his words, God was there with them in him, forgiving them. Forgiveness was an event in his relation with man the sinner from the first moment of his contact with him. The man knew himself accepted and, in being accepted, taken into a relationship that changed the very basis of his existence. The story of Jesus and Zacchaeus illustrates forgiveness as event in a personal relation prior to any verbal expression. Zacchaeus, the outsider, the tax gatherer, hated by his fellow country-men and excluded from their society, is represented as rad-ically transformed, not by any sermon or religious teach-ing, but by Jesus' words of greeting and acceptance: " Zacchaeus, come down, for I am going to stay with you today." Jesus' action of going into the homes of people like Zacchaeus and eating with them, so severely criticized by the official representatives of religion, was forgiveness in action, but what mystifies us is that both for him and for them it was not just the forgiveness of one man by an-other but *God's* forgiveness, cleansing and healing life to its very roots. Whether it was Jesus or the early church that formulated the phrase makes no difference; it de-scribes what happened in Jesus' relationship with men and women: " The Son of man has power on earth to forgive sins."

The two most dramatic forms of Jesus' healing ministry, so dramatic that a large amount of legendary material has become incorporated in the tradition, were instances of physical healing and of exorcism of demons. The validity of the basic tradition is guaranteed by the fact that both were continued in the early church's ministry as Paul knew it and wrote of it in his letters. Both unfortunately are open to perversion by being interpreted as though they had been effected by a kind of magical supernatural power. They must be understood, however, as concrete expres-sions of Jesus' mission to heal the rift in man's existence and reconcile him with God and man in a single act. Jesus made no claim to be able to heal any and every disease. He did not set himself up as a " faith healer." But he knew what psychosomatic medicine has established as fact to-day: many of the ailments from which men suffer have their source in hidden conflicts of man with himself or in the intimate relationships that constitute his life. He went

one step farther, though, and probing beneath the relation
of man to himself and to his fellows, found the source of
the trouble in the relation of man with God. Let healing
begin at the roots of life in the relation with God, and
healing would follow in the totality of life, both physically
and socially.

So also the enslavement of men to evil forces in and beyond themselves, which in the first century was thought of
as though a man were indwelt by an evil demon but which
in psychological terms we describe as a subjection to un-
desirable elements in our own subconscious being, was for
Jesus just another outcropping of the fundamental sickness
of man. Impelled by his very nature to seek the source of
his life not in himself but beyond himself, the man who no
longer has his life from God fastens upon some activity or
person or thing and constructs for himself a god or a panel
of gods. Whereas the true God in binding a man to himself
makes him free as never before, the man-made gods or
idols enslave him utterly. Demon possession was therefore
an emphatic sign of the absence of God from a man's life.
With the coming of the true God the false gods departed.
There were exorcists in those days who for a price would
liberate men from particular demons — for a time — and
their prosperity depended upon men continuing to fear and
to be enslaved by demons. Jesus' exorcism was of a very
different kind. It had in it no magical or supernatural ma-
nipulations. He restored men to the wholeness of their life
in unconditional openness to God so that like Paul, they
were freed of all fear that anything in heaven or earth
should ever again separate them from the source of their
life in God.

That Jesus' forgiveness should be experienced by men as
God's forgiveness, that his words should be heard as God's
words, that a divine authority should be felt in him before
which the demons lost their power over men, is not to be
explained by glibly asserting that, of course, Jesus was
God. It is forgotten that Jesus expected his disciples to ex-

ercise the same forgiveness, to preach and teach a gospel
that would be God's own word to men, and to be ministers
of the same reconciliation that he mediated. What God was
doing through his own mission Jesus expected to be continued in their mission. And there was no suggestion that
their humanity was in itself an obstacle. But the mystery remains why this amazing stream of forgiving, reconciling
love and power began its flow into human history in the
person of this Galilean Jew of the first century A.D. A clue
to the mystery is the fact that Christians were able to ful-
fill this ministry of reconciliation only when first the reconciliation was reality in themselves, only when first their
own alienation from God and man had been overcome and
they were " at one " with God. Their unanimous testimony
is that their reconciliation, their at-one-ment, was achieved
for them in the person of the Galilean Jew, in his ministry,
death, and resurrection. The strange power of his words,
of his forgiving love, of his death, lay in the perfect oneness of his being with God. He was in himself what all
men were created to be, the " Thou " to God's " I," the
image of God, the reflection of God's nature, the completely responsive servant of God's word, the unfailingly
obedient agent of God's purpose. In him man is at one with
God, and in his oneness with God he is the unveiling of the
goal of man's history. At the same time God is at one with
man in him, and through him is invading our humanity in
order to reconcile it to himself.

The danger at this point is that we may fail to grasp either the brutal depth of the problem of sin or the costliness
of oneness with God in an alienated world. Familiarity
with the prophets of Israel would warn us what to expect.
Putting themselves at the service of God's word to Israel
meant invariably having to cut directly across the established practices and attitudes of their people. In order to
be faithful to their task they had to be ready to be hated
and abused. Second Isaiah knew from his own painful experiences that to be at one with God in his purposes for

man was to be a human target for all the resistance and antagonism of man to God. A world that has established for itself what it considers a viable way of life does not take kindly to the question mark that the prophet sets against it in the name of God. It idealizes the values of the existing order and closes its eyes to the evils that undermine its life. So has it always been and so was it in Judaism in the first century. Therefore the yes of Jesus to God in its radicality was felt by the society of his time as an intolerable no to the values that it cherished. Jesus, in his uncompromising oneness with God, by his very being in the midst of men, exposed the depth of their alienation from God. One has only to think of the intensity with which an earnest and responsible religious man such as Paul at first hated him. Therefore, Jesus' primary work of reconciliation was not in his preaching and teaching but in his being what he was, in his perfect obedience to God, in his refusal under all the pressures that his contemporaries, including his disciples, exerted upon him to be other than an imaging of God's own loving purpose for man — which would tear the world apart to mend it. The cross on which he died is the symbol of how far he was willing to go in his obedience, that is, in his oneness with the purpose of God, so that the cross became the instrument through which his reconciling work continued in the years ahead.

The power of evil lies in its concealment. It enslaves men and makes them its agents only by blinding them, by presenting itself to them in a garment of virtue. Had anyone told Judas, even one short month before the crucifixion, that he would betray Jesus to his death, he would have been insulted and scandalized. He was a devoted disciple who already had begun to preach Jesus' gospel and who, like the others, had given up his former occupation to become a participant in the mission! The patriotism that eventually made him turn state's evidence against Jesus was not recognized by him as an evil that contradicted everything for which Jesus stood. So also Peter was still certain that nothing could shake his loyalty only a few hours before he, in order to protect himself, denied with oaths that he had ever known Jesus. Civilized Germans with their rich tradition of culture and religion could not bring themselves to believe that any countrymen of theirs would murder six million Jews or plunge the world into a destructive war. The majority of Americans are so certain of their nation's devotion to ideals of humanity that they cannot see what they are doing when with their colossal military forces they trample ruthlessly and needlessly on a tiny Asiatic people. But where man is made to stand before God, all concealment, blindness, and self-deception are at an end. The power of Jesus upon his cross to strip us naked and reveal us to ourselves is the power of his unbroken oneness with God, in the light of which we know our alienation and brokenness. In the presence of his obedience our disobedience can no longer be concealed, our pride is humbled, and we begin to recognize the depth of our need for the reconciliation that he has achieved and offered to us. Then and only then, when he has reconciled *us* to God, overcoming the alienation that has blinded us to what we are doing to our fellowmen, does Paul's statement begin to be reasonable and convincing that " God was in Christ reconciling the *world* unto himself."

10

Conversion

THE WORD that many people would expect to follow " sin "
is not " reconciliation " but " conversion." Especially in
America where so many churches had their origin and have
their increase in evangelistic revivals, there are large areas
where " conversion " is the key word. But there are equally
large areas where to speak of conversion is to embarrass
Christians. They disapprove of the emotionalism of evangelistic meetings, of the theology of most of the evangelists,
and of the kind of religiousness to which people are usually converted. In a land where most people have grown
up with at least some knowledge of the Christian faith,
conversion seems out of place to them except in extreme
instances of alienation from Christianity and the Christian
life. In both contexts a truth is concealed and lost which
is essential to Christian faith. We must begin with a criticism of both attitudes.

The evangelist is concentrated upon securing " decisions
for Christ " which he calls " conversions." Everything from
beginning to end — advance publicity, music, prayers, sermon, and a host of encouragers — is focused upon the
moment when he will exert himself to lift people out of
their seats and send them down the aisle to register their
decision. Certainly for many people who have never taken
their relationship with Jesus Christ seriously, this may be
the beginning of a new life. But it may also be conversion
to a narrow and highly opinionated form of religious self-

righteousness. The enthusiast for conversions rarely asks himself the question, Conversion to what? Christoph Blumhardt, of Bad Boll in Germany, who early in this century had a profound influence upon a wide range of Christian leaders, teaching them to take with a new seriousness the presence and power of God in Jesus Christ to transform human life in society as well as in individuals, refrained from all direct attempts to convert people. He feared that he might convert them to a " Blumhardt religion " rather than to a relationship with God through Jesus Christ which would set them in endless motion and carry them into regions uncharted by any Blumhardt. Some modern evangelists might well lay this to heart. People converted by a Billy Graham tend generally to adopt the theology and attitudes of Billy Graham rather than to be brought into a direct relation with the New Testament gospel which would awaken them to think for themselves and to be open to truth from whatever quarter it might come.

Many years ago a very conservative group of laymen planned a week of evangelistic meetings and requested the use of the church of which I was pastor. Their evangelist was notorious for his attacks on all the old-line churches. He had been expelled from his own denomination. He sponsored a very narrow and naïve theology. Yet these men were amazed that any Christian or any Christian church should refuse to cooperate with their project. " Are you not in favor of converting people? " they asked, and they had no understanding for the answer, " Not to the kind of unintelligent and contentious religiosity which your evangelist produces."

An equally important criticism has to do with the all-too-simple division of mankind into the converted and the unconverted. There have been in the past and perhaps still are some churches where for practical purposes the unconverted and the converted are seated in the auditorium with a clear line of demarcation between them. But even where the line is not made so directly visible, the division of man-

kind into the two compartments may be just as rigid.
"When were you converted and by whom?" the zealot
inquires, and if he detects any hesitancy to give the time
and place, he concludes at once that he has before him one
of the unconverted. But what have we here except a modernized version of the old Jewish division that was so intolerable to Jesus, the division between the righteous and
the sinners? Many of the attitudes of the Jewish "righteous" are reproduced in the Christian "righteous." Some
actually hold that by their conversion they have been completely freed of sin, and with sincerity make a claim of
righteousness attained that quite outdistances any Pharisee
of Jesus' day.

It is also disturbing that so often those Christians who
are most concerned with converting sinners and unbelievers are least concerned about social problems — economic
injustice, poverty, racial discrimination, aggressive nationalism. They would have the church confine its interest to
the "saving of souls," with the assurance that by christian-
izing the lives of individuals it will eventually christianize
society. Direct involvement in social, economic, and political problems seems to them unspiritual and a debasing
of the church. But they ignore the extent to which "converted" Christians in past and present have been guilty of
unawakened and unenlightened consciences in the face of
economic injustice and social prejudice. It is dangerous
and unbiblical to speak of the soul of man as though it
were a spiritual entity apart from his whole life in action
among his fellowmen. God's concern is with the whole
man, the social man, the man who makes political and economic decisions. Conversion is a fraud if its consequences
are confined to what is called "the spiritual life."

We need now to examine the opposite context in which
the word "conversion" is rarely heard. A distinguished
preacher in a great cathedral-like church one Sunday evening gave out as his theme, "How to Become a Christian."
The first half of the sermon was a clear and simple state-

ment of how God's grace in Jesus Christ meets man in his
weakness and confusion and transforms his life. Then the
preacher continued: " Of course, that is not the way in
which most of us who are here this evening became Christians. We were born into Christian homes. We were bap-
tized into membership in the church as infants. We grew
up in a Christian environment, never knowing a time when
we were not Christians. For us there was no need for conversion." He was expressing perfectly how a vast number
of church members feel about themselves. There was no
one moment before which they *were not* Christians and
after which they *were* Christians.

Although one must agree that all men do not become
Christians in the same way and certainly that the situation
of a person who has been nurtured from infancy in the
Christian faith is different from that of an outsider, the
dismissal of any need for conversion can easily become the
validation of a watered-down and emasculated form of
Christianity. Just as we asked, " What are they converted
to? " we have to ask, " What do they grow up into? " They
grow up into whatever version of the Christian faith happens to be established in their home and community, unless at some point they make contact with the gospel and
are forced out into new ways of thinking and acting — or
somewhere along the way their inherited religion is challenged, and unable to meet the challenge, they discard it.
The single most paralyzing element in the life of a church
is the extent to which its members have only the religion
and morality that they have inherited from the past.

Strangely now, our criticisms of this milieu in which
" conversion is not needed " fall into a pattern very similar
to our criticisms of the " converted." The pressure to conform to the beliefs and practices of the community is very
strong, and the refusal to conform may easily be interpreted as a rejection of Christianity. The person who begins to ask serious and searching questions in his endeavor
to understand the Christian faith may to his chagrin find

himself regarded with suspicion and distrust as a skeptic or an agnostic. In general, people find it much easier to conform if they do not think too deeply. It is taken for granted that those who conform and whose conformity is registered by their attendance in church (though this is not always necessary) are the Christians and that those who refuse to conform are the unbelievers. There is some caution about calling the nonconformists sinners. But here again, nevertheless, is a version of the ancient division of the community into righteous and sinners, insiders and outsiders, and the church is identified as the preserve of the righteous insiders. I inquired once of the minister of such a church why I never heard the word " repent " in his sermons, to which he replied: " I would be embarrassed to speak of repentance to these people in my congregation. They are the finest and most responsible people in the community. *They* are not the ones who need to repent. The people who need to repent never come inside my church." It is difficult for the minister of a respectable middle-class congregation, looking out at all those well-dressed, hard-working, decent, pleasant doctors, lawyers, businessmen, carpenters, housewives, to bring himself to address them as sinners desperately in need of the mercy of God — unless he has come close enough to them to know that each and every one of them in his own way is troubled with the same sickness that troubles the minister himself, the inability to be himself with integrity and consistency in all life's relationships! That is what the Christian only too often feels that he has to hide from his minister, from the members of his own family, and from himself.

All our thinking about " conversion " should start, not by attempting to define an experience by which a man becomes a Christian, but by asking what it means to respond in faith to the God who comes to us and offers himself to us in his word. There must be no narrowing of that word, separating the word that is heard in the person and mission of Jesus from the word to which prophets and apostles bear witness, nor can it be naïvely identified with Scripture as a whole, so that faith in response to God's word becomes " believing the Bible." We have to stand with the prophets, historians, psalmists, evangelists, and apostles and listen with them until we begin to hear the word they heard. " Faith comes by hearing and hearing by the word of God," said Paul. But the word of God is God himself in his word, God addressing himself to man, God offering himself to man, God conquering our sin and rebellion against him with his grace and forgiveness, God bridging the gulf that we have made between ourselves and him. As we saw earlier, this strange word that is at the heart of both Old and New Testaments, in which God calls man to find the fulfillment of his life in an intimate covenant relation with himself, has ever been a source of radical disturbance wherever it is heard, disturbing to the established order of society and disturbing to every fixed structure of religion and morality. The hearing of it makes man, like Abraham, a pilgrim on earth, haunted and drawn onward by the vision of what God intended and intends man's life to be. Therefore, the word of the prophets was ever a scathing judgment upon the people of Israel for whom the vision had faded and left them blind to the inhuman conditions in which many Israelites lived. And the word that men heard from Jesus and in him, claiming them for a life of unconditional openness to both God and man, was a scathing judgment on the narrow, self-righteous religiousness of the men of his day.

God's word, in Old and New Testament alike, can never be heard except as both judgment and promise for us in our present condition of life. Because in it God himself draws near to us, it lays bare our distance from him, our resistance to his will, our indifference to his purposes for us and for our world. The hearing of God's word makes us stand naked under his judgment, and if we are unwilling to be stripped naked in his presence, we cannot hear the word of infinite promise and mercy which is inseparable from the word of judgment. God's No! to what we are, his rejection of all that is false in us, is intrinsic to his acceptance of us as his children. Thus, Jesus Christ in his perfect humanity is God's judgment upon our inhumanity as individuals and upon the inhumanity of our societies, but in the same moment he is the promise of a new humanity.

There can, then, be no hearing of the word of God, no openness to Jesus Christ, without conversion. The word " conversion " needs to be lifted out of its evangelistic context and restored to its proper place as what we expect to happen in our lives from the hearing of God's word.

Where a man's ears have been closed to that word and his life set in a directly contradictory direction, the first hearing may be like a sudden explosion that turns everything upside down. Faith may be born in a single dramatic confrontation, as it was for Paul (although even for him what he had already heard from the Old Testament Scriptures was an important background for his conversion). Or faith may be the product of a succession of responses as the witness of prophets and apostles is heard more and more clearly, and because no one of them is sudden, the believer does not think of them as conversions. But they *are* conversions, for it is impossible to live in the communion of the saints (prophets, apostles, and all who point us beyond ourselves to God) and open to their witness without being daily humbled in repentance under God's judgment and renewed by his forgiveness. The word of God is *daily* bread, the bread by which alone man lives. To hear it is to die daily to the past and to receive each day really new from the hand of God. There is no room for self-righteousness in such a faith. The word of God takes care of that. Self-righteousness is possible only for those who have somehow silenced the word in which God brings all men under judgment and convicts them of their sin. Ironically, self-righteousness is invariably a demon-

stration of deafness to the word of God even in those who
passionately protest their devotion to the Scriptures. No
man, as long as he lives, can hear the voice of God and fail
to say with Isaiah, " Woe is me for I am undone, for I am
a man of unclean lips and I dwell in the midst of a people
of unclean lips," or more simply with the tax gatherer of
Jesus' parable, " Lord, be merciful to me a sinner." Even
the most earnest Christian to his dying day has no access
to the grace and mercy of God except as the sinner that
he is.

11

Word

SOME READERS may have found it exasperating that the "word" of God has had such a prominent place in our discussion without ever being clearly defined. Some may even feel an element of unfair coercion in the use of the term itself. Does it not silence all human words when appeal is made to a word *of God?* Have we not already had all too many instances in history of men imposing their religious viewpoint, and with it perhaps also their political and economic viewpoints, upon other men, and using as their incontestable authority the agreement of their various convictions with the word of God himself? We are quick to detect this in the fundamentalist who asserts the inerrancy of Scripture and then transfers the inerrancy to his own religious teachings which he claims to have based firmly on Scripture. But can we be quite sure that even though we make no claim of inerrancy either for Scripture or for our own teachings, we are not in some degree confusing our words with God's word in order to lend them authority? We cannot leave the question there. We must not shrink from asking it also concerning those who, first in Israel, then in the early church, with evident sincerity were certain that they spoke for God. Were they, too, claiming for their particular insights an unwarranted authority when they led men to expect to hear from their lips nothing less than the word of God himself?

The question is particularly acute in our modern age because we are more aware than the people of any earlier age that all things human change and pass away. Only in the last century has man begun to grasp the dimensions of his history and that to be a man is to be in a process of becoming. Not so long ago he was content to think of his world and of his history as beginning in 4004 B.C., the date that he found in the margin of the King James version of the Bible, but now he has to cope with a universe that reaches back hundreds of millions of years and a human history that can be traced by the archaeologists some hundreds of thousands of years. Abraham, who once seemed to stand close to the beginning of human history, has to be seen now as comparatively a latecomer. Traces have been found at Jericho in Palestine of a community that dates nearly 2500 years earlier than Abraham, and flourishing civilizations of that earlier age have been uncovered in Egypt and Mesopotamia. The story of Israel now unfolds for us, not in lonely isolation, but in the lively context of a wide range of ancient cultures — Canaanite, Egyptian, Hittite, Assyrian, Babylonian, Persian, and Greek. More important still has been our recognition of an unceasing historical development in Israel and in the early Christian church. There was a time when the Bible was read as though it were all of a piece, but that time is no longer. As the historical setting of each writing has been ferreted out and defined for us, the words have taken on new meaning, and we have become aware of the various stages that can be traced in the faith of Israel and in the faith of the early Christian church. The Bible, far from being a collection of static truths, identical in quality regardless of their time and place of origin, is the record of a dynamic movement in which men had constantly to change their minds and their practices or be left behind.

The most striking and relevant feature of the Biblical story for our present consideration, then, is the refusal of those who form the unifying core of the history to freeze the movement at any one point, as though at that point they had the word of God complete. There is always more to come, more truth to be revealed, more life to be realized. The prophet who declares the word of God to his people does not permit them to absolutize either his words or those of the prophets who preceded him but rather points them toward a future for which all that has been known thus far is but a preparation and a promise. Never is his word the last word, and never does he feel it necessary to make his words agree in every detail with what his predecessors have spoken. The relation between Jesus and John the Baptist illustrates forcefully the contrast between a dynamic and a static conception of the word of God. Some followers of John could not understand why Jesus, who recognized in John a true prophet of God, did not make his teachings and his practices conform to those of John. How could the word of God for Jesus be different from the word of God for John? Jesus answered them, " Wisdom [i.e., a Hebrew synonym for " word of God "] is justified in all her children," by which he meant that every servant of God's truth must be free to bear his witness in his own way and that if he merely made his words and practices conform to those of John, he would be unfaithful to the truth itself.

Some of Jesus' disciples tried to do with Paul what the disciples of John had attempted with Jesus. Jesus had limited his mission with few exceptions to the " lost sheep of the house of Israel," Jews in Palestine who were untouched by the ministrations of the synagogue; therefore Paul was deemed to be unfaithful to Jesus in taking the gospel freely to the Gentiles. Jesus had all his life conformed to Jewish religious practices which were not in contradiction to his understanding of the will of God; therefore Paul was expected to require of his Gentile converts that they become Jews and conform at least in some measure to Jewish practices. Those who thought in this way may well have been offended also that the gospel as Paul preached it sounded in its terminology so different from what they had heard from

Jesus. But Paul had no interest in imitating Jesus. His unity
with him was at a deeper level. Just as Jesus knew himself
at one with John the Baptist in spite of all the differences
between them, so Paul knew himself at one with Jesus. He
had no other aim than that the life and mission of Jesus
should be renewed in him, not imitated but renewed.

The first major attempt to freeze the word of God in
static form took place in Judaism under Greek influence.
The Greeks, whose culture pervaded the Middle East for
more than three centuries before the time of Jesus, had sacred writings of their own, the works of Homer and Hesiod,
and they taught that every word in these books was directly inspired by the gods and inerrantly true. To question their truth was an offense against the gods themselves
and an imperiling of the community. Could the Jews whose
prophets through the centuries had spoken in the name of
God and as his messengers make any lesser claim for their
sacred writings? The days of the prophets lay far in the
past. The word of God was now to be heard not from the
lips of a living prophet but from the pages of a book. The
words of the book became so identified with the word of
God that the distance between the human words and the
word to which they witnessed was quite forgotten. From
that it was but a short step to the absolutizing of both the
sacred writings and the religious order that ostensibly was
based upon them. The last word had been spoken, and all
the words of God were now in man's possession in the sacred writings (and for some, in the equally sacred unwritten tradition). There was no longer any room for a word
from God which would in any way set in question what
was already established — no room for a prophet such as
John the Baptist, no room for Jesus Christ!

The Fourth Gospel, whose author had thought so deeply
concerning the nature of the word of God, dealt incisively
with this problem. Jesus, in his confrontation with the
spokesmen for Judaism, is represented as challenging their
practice of identifying the words of Scripture directly with

the word of God. " You search the Scriptures diligently, supposing that in them you have eternal life; yet, although their testimony points to me, you refuse to come to me for that life." (John 5:39.) When the truth of God to which the whole Old Testament was one continuous witness was there before them in the words and person of Jesus, they were blind to it and could not recognize it. " If you believed Moses [i.e., the Pentateuch, which was regarded as the most sacred of all Scripture], you would believe what I tell you." (V. 46.) The all-important distinction is made here between the Scriptures as *witness* to the word of God and the word itself. The truth is not at man's disposal in a set of human words so that he can master it and bend it to his purposes. Rather, the words point him to a reality in his own immediate circumstances, a command and promise, a judgment and a justification, before which he must bend in humility, mastered and set free to live. And even the words of Jesus himself are not the final words of truth. The promise is given by him to his disciples on the last night of his earthly life that the Holy Spirit will lead them into all truth, and more than once the author of this Gospel states that only after the resurrection of Jesus did his disciples rightly understand what he had been saying. The word heard in the past has to be illuminated by the word heard in the present, or like the manna in the desert, it ceases to be the bread of life.

It is clear, then, that there is no simple answer to the question, What is this word of God which is so central? The directness of the prophets with their " Thus saith the Lord," and their manner of speaking as though it were not Isaiah or Jeremiah but God himself who addresses Israel, may conjure up an image of conversations of God with men. This is accentuated by traditions that portray God in dialogue with the patriarchs or with Job. And behind these traditions and the manner of prophetic address undoubtedly lie ecstatic visions and auditions such as those of Moses, Isaiah, and Paul, in which God is seen as fire or

light or as a majestic heavenly monarch and his presence
is apprehended in specific words. But elsewhere we are
warned against too literal or naïve a concept of the
" word." In Genesis, God's word is his action; he speaks
and the world comes into being. In the Fourth Gospel the
word is God himself in his love for his world, invading its
darkness with his light and offering to every man life that
has no death in it. Jesus in his person is the Incarnate
Word, the word in its ultimate embodiment, expressed in
his words but much more powerfully in his actions and in
what he suffered at the hands of men. The " word " is
" God with man," just as faith is " man with God." But
God with man is a personal relation, and like all personal
relations it is sustained in freedom by the speaking and
hearing of words. What God is to us has meaning only
when it is expressed in words and signs, and what we are
to God demands expression also in words and signs. It is
no accident that signs have so much prominence in the sus-
taining of communion with God, for the mystery of personal relation is of a depth that reaches out beyond all
that can be comprehended in human words.

Another important aspect of the " word " looms up
when we consider how inseparable it is in the Old Testament from God's action in history. God's word to man dis-
closes what God is doing in man's history. This is just another way of saying that God is not absent from man in
some distant region but is with him in the concrete situations of his daily life. Greek and Hindu religions despair of
finding meaning in the events of time and teach men to
seek God beyond the world and history. But the God of
Israel and the God and Father of Jesus Christ meets man
not beyond history but in history. He chooses men as his
dwelling place, and in his word he reveals himself to them
as confronting them in everything that happens and in every
relationship of life. He meets us in the brother who claims
our time and understanding. He meets us in the events that
make up our day. That is what men are so slow to believe.

They dismiss God to a distant heaven where he may be worshiped in comparative safety and they lock up his word in a book which they reverence but do not try to understand. Then they wonder why in spite of their religion there is no meaning for them either in their personal history or in the history of their world! The word to which the Scriptures witness in all their manifold richness, the word that comes closest to us in the personal history of Jesus Christ, fulfills its purpose only when it is for us the unveiling of God's presence with us now in the events of our existence and in its every unveiling a confrontation with a life-or-death decision. We do not meet our God apart from life but in the midst of life. Our meeting with him will be in darkness and confusion, however, unless our ears are open to the word that he has spoken and still speaks.

12

Church

WE ARE painfully slow to grasp that the primary witness to the word of God is not in a book but in persons. When Moses heard the voice of God, he did not go home and write a book. He went back to Egypt and called a motley and most unpromising group of slaves to rise up out of their slavery and become the people of God. The word created a community and set it marching into an uncharted future. Centuries later the traditions in which the community commemorated its birth became a written record through which the later community, remembering its origin, was recalled to its purpose.

The word of the prophets, sounding into the life of an Israel that was becoming as unjust, as greedy, as inhuman in its relationships as any of the surrounding nations, called into existence an Israel within Israel that was humbled by the word it heard and let itself be given a new heart. It was this Israel within Israel that cherished and preserved the messages of the prophets.

Jesus did all his writing in persons and left behind not one scrap of manuscript. He knew the danger of the living word of God becoming locked up in the pages of a sacred book. Therefore his endeavor was to implant his gospel in a community of disciples, an Israel within Israel again, and what arrested the attention of men in that ancient world was, first of all, the unique life that was lived in the community of disciples in response to what Jesus had been, and was still, to them.

So also Paul, when the truth of his gospel was challenged at Corinth, did not argue about words but pointed, rather, to the life that had been created in the Christian community in Corinth as a consequence of his gospel. " You are the letter [of commendation] that we need, a letter written on your heart; any man can see it for what it is and read it for himself. . . . It is plain that you are a letter that has come from Christ, given to us to deliver. A letter written not with ink but with the Spirit of the living God."

It is still true today that the primary witness to the word of God is not in a book but in persons. We have far too much confidence in the Bible as a sacred book which of itself is able to do all that is needful. In America alone more than eight million copies of the Bible are purchased each year. We are flooded with Bibles. Yet there is a famine in the land so far as the word of God is concerned. Nothing is more difficult to find than persons in whose words we hear a word from God that stands recognizably in continuity with the word to which the prophets and apostles bear their witness. But let us be honest with ourselves: nothing is more difficult for us ourselves, nothing shakes us to the depths of our being so radically, as to have the task, in continuity with prophets and apostles, of speaking the word of God to our fellowmen. It is not enough for our church or for our nation that there are a hundred million Bibles somewhere in the land. The word to which the Bible witnesses demands a living witness now, words spoken in utter integrity in witness to the one word, through which the Spirit of God will write afresh in men's hearts, create Christ anew in them, and make them the responsive instrument of his purpose in the present-day world. The life of the community which the gospel creates is the indispensable interpreter of the gospel itself. Words read from a book or heard from a pulpit have no power until they are magnified and have their meaning driven home by being lived out in the everyday life of a community. We are aware that the truth

of God searches our hearts and convinces us most powerfully when it meets us in the person of Jesus, incarnated in
him in his life and death. Why then do we not see that it is
intrinsic to the nature of the truth of God that it has to be
embodied in persons, not just in the one person Jesus, but
in the community of persons who owe to him all that they
are, his church?

Our difficulty in defining the church is that we are familiar with so many churches. What the churches *are* blinds
us to what the church *is*. This is not a blanket accusation
against the existing churches that they have so falsified
their nature that they are ready to be scrapped and thrown
on the ash heap of history. There has been far too much of
that kind of talk already, driving people away from the
churches and discouraging men from entering the ministry.
When we criticize the church as we have known it, far too
often we forget that we would have no knowledge of Jesus
Christ, no standing ground from which to criticize the
church, had not the church in spite of all its failings borne
a faithful witness to us somewhere and somehow. In simple
ways God preserves a witness to his gospel so that there remains an Israel within Israel, a church within the church.
But the church within the church is often hidden, just as
the Israel within Israel was often hidden by the official institutions of the nation.

A group of young people at a summer conference, all of
them devoted and active members of their home churches,
undertook a study of the church in the New Testament.
Their first surprise was to find the earliest Christians in serious confusion and controversy concerning both the definition of a Christian and the dimensions of the church's
task. They had expected a model church, not one struggling with problems like their own. As the story of the
church's beginnings unfolded before their eyes they were
even more amazed: Jesus' molding a fellowship of disciples with whom he could share not just his mission but the
very life that he had in God; the slowness of those disciples

who were closest to him to understand him both in his life-time and beyond his death and resurrection; their unreadi-ness to be his church until the same Spirit of God that was the source of his power took possession of them; the mira-cle of transformation as those few disciples, open to the presence and power of God in the gospel, became the nu-cleus of a worldwide mission. The reaction of the young people was, " This is not the church as we have known it." What they knew was a congregation of reasonably good-living people who worshiped together once each week and engaged in various kinds of church activities but who were not at all interested in being disciples, students of their faith, or in sharing either Jesus' mission or his rather dan-gerous life in God. The idea of a God who is no longer at a distance but who through his word and Spirit makes men his dwelling place and uses them as his means of getting on with his purpose for humanity, or at least for their particu-lar corner of humanity, was unfamiliar. The first impulse of the students was to sit in judgment upon their home churches, as though they had been lifted out of those churches into some superior position by what they had learned from the New Testament, instead of recognizing their involvement and responsibility for the church as it is and that God through the Scriptures was calling them to be the church within the church. The renewal of the church has always come not from without but from within, not from those who in despair or disgust have abandoned it but from those who, with their eyes open to all that is wrong with it, have known themselves called to follow the much more difficult alternative — of being the church.

It would do much to dispel our illusions and misconcep-tions about the church if in a single volume there were sketched quite simply the story of the " people of the word " from its first beginnings in the mists of early Hebrew his-tory down through the Kingdoms of Israel and Judah, the Dispersion, the centuries of Judaism, the revolutionary birth within Judaism of the Christian church, then its invasion and conquest of the Greco-Roman world, and all the changes through which it has passed from then until now. Unfortunately, we usually get the story only in bits and pieces. We fail to see it in its massive and, one is tempted to say, miraculous continuity. Civilizations are born, flourish, and pass away, but no matter how colossal the disasters, this " people of the word " survives. The history does not tempt us to glorify the church as though its survival were the product of its strength and virtue. Rather, with Second Isaiah, we are inclined to say of the church in every age, " called of God from the beginning " (Isa. 49:1) and " a transgressor from the beginning " (ch. 48:8). We have but to look into three crises in the church's life, centuries apart, which were met by Jeremiah, Paul, and Luther to recognize that the church survived only because men's ears were opened once again to hear the word which, when it bursts forth afresh, is like a conqueror conscripting men for his service.

The church's temptation has ever been to forget that it is en route under sealed orders toward a distant destination, and, settling down upon some one point in history, to make itself at home. There is a tendency in human nature to feel concerning any religious order, practices, or ideas, once they have become established and familiar, that they should be unchanging and eternal. What drives men to despair in many congregations is the amount of energy required to achieve the smallest changes, the rigidity of attitudes on all matters great and small, the complacency of people in responsible positions about structures that have long ago outlived their reason for existence, the tenacity with which they continue to think and talk about the problems of yesterday rather than the problems of today. But if the church is the servant of the word in which God reveals what he is doing at this moment in our history, not what he was doing yesterday or two hundred years ago, but now, and if faithfulness means putting ourselves at the service of God that he may get on with his work, then there should be a readiness in the church to respond in each moment to God's bidding and direction, even as a well-trained army responds instantly to its commander. The very character of the church's relation to the word in which it has its creative source demands of it a mobility, a readiness to march, a willingness to obey the commands of God. The church's most tragic sins of disobedience have always been the product not of reckless and foolhardy ventures but of complacent acquiescence to the established order.

The most recent illustration of the power of the gospel to shake a church loose from its rigid structures and set it in motion again has, of course, been the Roman Catholic Church. Changes have taken place almost overnight in the relations between Catholics and Protestants which open up tremendous possibilities for the future. Frequently, the changes are attributed wholly to the influence of Pope John and the Vatican Council called by him, and nothing can detract from the honor due this most remarkable man. But neither Pope John nor the Vatican Council could have achieved what they did had not Biblical scholarship in the Roman Church been liberated from its former restraints in 1943 by a papal encyclical, so that the Scriptures came open in a new way and the gospel to which they witness asserted its authority over the minds and hearts of archbishops, bishops, priests, scholars, and the people at large. A word was heard that had to be obeyed, and that obedience set the church in motion.

There are three necessities in the life of a pilgrim church: continuity with its past, especially with that decisive period of its past that is canonized in Scripture; openness and readiness to act at God's command in the present; and willingness to face a future that will render all the formulas of past and present insufficient. The genius of a truly Biblical faith is that it keeps all three in balance. But let any one element be lacking and the result is fatal. The conservative tendency in the church has been to emphasize continuity with the past at the expense of openness to the present and future, with the result that the church becomes anchored to some one period of the past and paralyzed. The liberal tendency has been to emphasize openness to the present and future at the expense of continuity with the past, with the result that the church in its rootlessness is in danger of merely echoing the most impressive voices and movements of the contemporary world. Tradition and mobility may seem at first to be in essence contradictory, but in the life of the church they are complementary. The church with mobility but ignorant of its tradition keeps making all the mistakes of the past over again, and the church with a rich tradition but no mobility becomes the prisoner of its tradition. We look back, but only to recover our direction ever afresh as we move forward through the changing present into the unknown future.

13

Hope

HOPE IS ACCORDED a very minor place in the thinking of most Christians. Yes, of course, a Christian must be hopeful, always taking the more cheerful view of things and never giving way needlessly to discouragement. An optimistic outlook is widely recommended. But Christian hope is something much deeper and wider than just a sunny outlook on tomorow. Christian hope has to do with the goal of history and the goal of personal existence. Is human life no more than a candle that flickers and burns for a few years, giving off its light, and then is snuffed out forever, or is it a movement of life toward a destination, with every step and every decision of gravest importance, even though the destination cannot be reached within our brief span of time? Is history just a restless movement of neurotic human beings, haunted by dreams of a life that might one day be attained and struggling ever upward toward it only to be plunged downward by strange and uncontrollable destructive forces in their natures, or has it all a goal toward which it moves in spite of clumsy flounderings to and fro? More important than either of these questions is the question mark that the Christian hope sets against the whole of our existence. It says to us: " If the humanity revealed in Jesus Christ is in truth your goal, then what are you doing settling down in that compromising mixture of humanity and inhumanity which is your present self? And if you really mean it when you pray for the Kingdom of God to come on earth, the Kingdom for which Jesus lived and died, how do you so complacently accept an ordering of human society that leaves so many millions hungry, naked, homeless, ignorant, and robbed of their opportunity for life? "

Christian hope is no minor aspect of the gospel. It may have puzzled us why Paul included hope with faith and love as one of the three gifts that endure when all else has passed away, but for Paul it was no mystery. There could be no openness of the human self to God without a faith that in each moment was responding in obedience to God's command or without a love for God and man that was a reflection in human life of God's own love. Man standing before God had to confess in honesty the disobedience that was ever mingled with his obedience and the self-centeredness that warred against his love. The Christian was a realist who did not conceal from himself the sin and the unbelief in which his life was still to some degree enmeshed, but the sin and unbelief no longer had their power to enslave and paralyze. Their power was broken once and for all when Jesus offered unto God his perfect obedience. Therefore, the Christian whose life by faith was bonded together with the life of Christ lived henceforward in the strength of that victory. In Christ was revealed to him the life for which he was created and which would one day be his own. A hope was born in him that reached out beyond all the limitations of time and mortality.

We need to ask, then, why the Christian hope today commands so little interest. When the World Council of Churches took as its theme " Christ — The Hope of the World " for its meeting in Evanston in 1954, there was consternation and even derision in many Christian circles in America. It seemed to them irresponsible to focus attention upon the future rather than upon the urgent and practical problems of the present. It was significant, however, that European representatives who in the postwar world had been ministering to people who despaired of a future for humanity found the theme more practical than any other. A number of factors have combined to create the American disinterest. The Second Coming of Christ predicted in Scripture has become the dominant interest of sects such as the Jehovah's Witnesses which use the Scriptures to construct a timetable of future events and manage to have Christ at the final stage install them as rulers of the world! So also the hope of immortality has become to such a degree a belief that if you are good, you go on and on that it has lost the interest and respect of thoughtful people. More important, though, in America as in Russia, there has been a secularizing of the Christian hope. In its place we have the good or great society in which poverty, prejudice, ignorance, and all the other sources of human unhappiness will have been overcome — and one has no need of Christian faith to be confident that we are on the way toward the goal. The decline of Christian socialism in recent years is an indication of the advance of this process of secularization. Something similar has happened to the personal hope. The confidence has grown that man has now at his disposal knowledge that should enable him to come to self-fulfillment by his own adjustment of his relationships to the world, to the people round about him, and to himself. He has no need of God or immortality. The validity of these forms of hope we need not examine here. It is sufficient to suggest that consciously or unconsciously they have frequently substituted themselves for the Christian hope and removed its relevance for the future. Man has taken his future firmly in his own two hands.

A very real difficulty in understanding the Christian hope as it is expressed in Scripture is the seemingly fantastic imagery in which it is cast. An era dawns in which men make plowshares of their swords and the fierce lion becomes as harmless as a lamb. God himself is pictured marching through the earth like a mighty warrior, conquering his enemies and establishing a just order for all men. In the Gospels there is attributed to Jesus a prediction of wars, earthquakes, famines, and persecutions, during which the gospel is to be preached to all nations. Then after more distresses the light will fade from sun, moon, and stars, and the Son of Man will appear riding on the clouds and sending his angels across the world to gather his chosen people. Paul anticipates a final assault of evil when a man who incarnates in himself the power of evil will usurp the authority of God, but Christ in his second coming will destroy him and, gathering together the faithful of all the ages, will never be separated from them again. For some people it is an embarrassment also that Jesus and Paul, like Second Isaiah in the Old Testament, speak at times as though they expected history to reach its end at any moment and God's direct rule replace all existing forms of government.

We can only be confused if we take all the imagery and predictions quite literally, and we shall most likely miss the hope that is hidden in them. We need to realize that whereas the Hebrews and the early Christians had a keen sense of history so far as it was a recounting of their own past, they were without anything of our knowledge of world history, and they did not, like us, think of the future as history that has not yet been lived. Conscious as we are of those hundreds of thousands of years behind us, we quite easily envisage an endless succession of years ahead. Not so the Hebrews. Under the guidance of the prophets they saw the past not primarily as a complex of human thoughts and actions but as the story of God's dealings with his people Israel, in which was revealed a purpose that he had for his whole creation and for all mankind. History was meant to move toward a goal. The meaning of man's life on earth was the realization of a human community in which the very nature of God himself would be reflected in the relationships of his people. The essence of evil was man's rebellion against that purpose of God and his building, instead, communities that were unjust and inhuman. By such rebellion he brought destruction upon himself and delayed the fulfillment of God's plan. But it was inconceivable that God should be defeated. The sovereignty of God in his world meant the sovereignty of truth, faithfulness, justice, and love and their eventual triumph over all the forces that stood against them. Therefore, the Hebrew prophet saw the future not as centuries of human history yet to come but wholly in terms of the completion of God's purpose for man, sometimes darkly as an overshadowing judgment on man's evil in order to conquer his rebellion, sometimes joyously heralding the dawn of the days of fulfillment. Both visions of the future were the product of an unshakable confidence in a purpose of God for Israel in which God refuses to let himself be defeated. Looking back on their history they see God at work, disciplining them in the dark days of judgment, carrying them forward in the bright days of promise and faithfulness, but always moving them toward the goal of his gracious purpose for them. The idea of history as movement toward such a goal had its origin with the Hebrews, and it was born of their faith in God's intention for man. The Greeks had no such idea but saw history as movement in a circle. When man becomes the center of the world and takes history into his own hands, perhaps it is inevitable that his history should become movement in a circle rather than progress toward a goal.

Perhaps now we can see why the prophet's passionate hatred of all injustice, oppression, and irresponsibility was a product of his hope. What was most wrong in man's inhuman conduct was his opposition to God's loving purpose for his whole creation. To hope and to pray for God's Kingdom to come on earth is to stand ready to resist the destructive forces — war, poverty, prejudice, hatred, ignorance, and greed — that are barriers in the way of God's fulfillment of his purpose.

Although the Christian hope generates an active opposi-

tion to such evils, it also delivers the believer from the
frustration of a utopianism that expects the final victory
over evil tomorrow. It gives him patience. He is not driven
to despair either by the severity of his own continuing
struggle with the problem of evil or by the immensity of
the destructive forces that threaten the future of mankind.
God takes time to win his victories, and sometimes what
seem to be defeats, as at the cross, turn out to be the
greatest victories of all. So also with the church — the
honest Christian is not surprised to find in it unresolved
contradictions with which he is already familiar in himself. He and the church alike have to work out their salvation in history, and at no one point does God expect com-
pleteness, only faithfulness. Only in Jesus Christ has the
church as yet offered a perfect obedience to God and
Israel been truly Israel, and what we see in him becomes
the goal of all our hopes and our endeavors.

When man — American man or Russian man — substitutes his great society for God's Kingdom as the object
of his hope, no longer is the established order shaken by
being seen under the judgment of God's design and God's
command, but rather, a corrupt society conceals from
itself what it is by clothing itself in the nobility of its ideals.
It keeps its eyes so firmly fixed upon its high intentions
that it can no longer see the horror of what it is actually
doing. So also the man who has become competent to ad-
just all his relationships in such a way as to secure his
self-fulfillment has committed himself to a philosophy of
urbane self-centeredness, unaware that man's self-sovereignty is the very root of his perennial failure to be human.

What, then, of the Christian hope for the individual? It
is no cheap confidence in a vague something beyond
death with which to quiet the fear of dissolution. It is
rooted and grounded in the nature of God, in the faith that
God does not let himself be defeated even by death, that
what he begins he finishes. Paul says, " He that hath begun
a good work in you will complete it." In Jesus Christ, God

has revealed his intention for us, the life for which he has
destined us, to be made in his own image. Not even for
Paul was that goal reached within his lifetime. To our very
dying day we " press toward the mark," being changed
from likeness to likeness that we may be made like him.
Is death the final victor and not life? Is death stronger
than God? Or can God be trusted to finish what he has
begun? Does the great adventure reach on beyond the gates
of death? If we have a really Christian hope of immortality, it is based not on what we are but on what God
can do and has promised to do. The promise is Jesus
Christ and he seals the promise with his Spirit.

14

Predestination

IT IS QUESTIONABLE whether the word " predestination " should be allowed to remain in the Christian vocabulary. It is so loaded with false meanings that one wonders whether it can ever be rehabilitated. And yet it is there in people's minds, especially in the minds of Presbyterians, as a Biblical word and concept which rouses either their rebellion or their fascination. Also, unless we come upon a better word, it continues to mark a highly important area of our faith and our existence, the relation of the things that happen to the unfolding of our destiny, the question of what God is doing with us in the motley of events which make up our history. One can see at once that predestination is not a concept that can stand alone. Looming up behind it is the Biblical doctrine of God as Creator of the world and Lord of history. Shining through it is the conviction of the prophets that Israel's liberation from Egypt to become a nation and the sequence of events by which its destiny was shaped were not the strokes of genius of charismatic leaders but the works in history of a God who for his own reasons had a care for them. The cross comes into the picture — tragic accident or act of God for man's redemption?

We can dismiss at once as unbiblical and unchristian the superficial but widespread meaning of the word, that all events are fated to happen exactly as they do. Soldiers frequently draw comfort and courage from this conviction.

The day and hour of their deaths is fixed so that neither they nor the enemy can alter it. But it can also be used to escape the pain of responsibility for what we have done: we tell ourselves, looking back, that we seemed to have been flung headlong into the action as though we were fated to do it and could not resist. We would be wiser to contemplate the close relation between inward character and outward action than to throw responsibility for what we have done on a God or fate beyond ourselves. The surest indication that we have of what we are is in what we do, and our blindness to ourselves is such that we shrink from taking full responsibility for our actions. That fatalism has strong attractions is evident in the popularity of astrological literature — booklets on the newsstands that sell in the thousands, columns in the newspapers — little changed since the days of ancient Babylon and Rome. Our natures are determined by the constellation of the stars when we were born! Our destinies in every particular were fixed from the beginning and nothing we do can change them! This is pure paganism and the very antithesis to a Christian faith.

Neither in the Old Testament nor in the New does God fix destinies or events from the beginning so that what happens in time is unalterable. The very essence of man's life as he comes forth from the hand of God is that he has freedom to choose between alternatives. God has no interest in puppets but only in free persons, for freedom is essential to a personal relation, and the purpose of human existence is fellowship with God and with the fellowman. The God of Israel is not a distant monarch who determines the events of history from the beginning and then lets them unroll; he is with his people in the midst of the history, burdened by their oppressions or by their blindness and rejoicing in their obedience, warning them of the way that leads to death and pleading with them to choose the way to life. The covenant relation between God and Israel, with its closest analogies in the relations of husband and wife

or father and child, is one of action and response with no
room in it for any fatalism.

So also in the New Testament, faith is not submission
to whatever happens or acceptance of our present selves
as fixed and unchangeable, but rather, response to a word
we hear in Jesus Christ which promises us deliverance
from our present broken selves into a new life with God
in which the meaning of everything that happens will be
transformed. Far from counseling submission to the ills
and misfortunes of life, Jesus made men rebels against a
social order that generated bitter hatreds, against religious
customs and prejudices that prevented men from being
human with one another, against callousness toward any
form of human failure. Far from accepting the established
order as the will of God, Jesus challenged it so sharply that
everyone in authority wanted him silenced. And in the
succeeding years his followers were never accused of being submissive. On the contrary, they were constantly sus-
pected of being dangerous revolutionists because of the
way in which their faith seemed to turn the world upside
down.

Not only humanists but also some Christian theologians
of our time have found it necessary to relieve God of all
involvement in the things that happen. The universe is
seen by them as a vast impersonal environment that rolls
on its way through its millions of years in complete indifference to man and his fate. History then takes on
something of this impersonal character too. It is in part a
sequence of accidents, and insofar as it has meaning, the
meaning is wholly the product of man's initiative. Man
must free himself, therefore, from the illusion that events
in history are in any way the works of God with some
transcendent and cosmic meaning in them and must recognize that he, man, has the responsibility for the shaping
of history. It is in his hands to make of it what he will.
It is not something that happens to him and of which he
then has to puzzle out the meaning; it is the product of

his intentions and of his passions.

The humanist may cast this world view in a godless form, inciting man to courage in the face of a universe that is careless of his existence and encouraging him to explore, to enjoy, and to augment those treasures of the mind and spirit and those amenities of civilized living which alone make man's brief span of life bearable. The theologian who goes partway with the humanist is less confident of the ability of man to achieve a meaningful existence. There is the fatal defect of man's dividedness within himself, his imprisonment in his past, in an inauthentic self, and his powerlessness to reach out and claim his authentic future. He has to hear a word from God in which God's love will meet him and, freeing him from his past, open to him a new self and a new future. Therefore, he listens at that point in history where the Christian gospel came to birth, and he hears a word from God that sets him on his way toward his self-fulfillment. But it is self-fulfillment in a world that is not God's world and can never be man's home and in a history that has no destination and is no more than the temporary environment which he and others can provide for their own self-fulfillment.

The question, then, that the concept of predestination sets out to answer is what relation there is between the God who meets us in his word and the outward events that make up our history. When we call him " sovereign in his power," what kind of control over the things that happen are we attributing to him? We have already seen that it is directly contrary to the Biblical understanding of the relation between God and man to think of God as exercising direct control. Also, it makes of him a monster of cruelty and of man a helpless victim. And yet there is abundant evidence in literature and life of how widely this naïve view of God's omnipotence has created false expectations and soul-destroying bitterness. " Why did God do this to me? " " If God is sovereign, why does he let such ghastly things happen? " It is surprising to find men of eminent intelligence quoting the old saw concerning God, " If loving, not omnipotent; if omnipotent, not loving," as though it impaled the Christian faith on the horns of an insoluble dilemma. It does not seem to occur to them that *divine* omnipotence may take another form than direct control of the things that happen.

The omnipotence of God and his sovereignty over the events of history can never be understood by us until we face the full implications of the crucifixion of Jesus and of his conviction that somehow in his death the will of God was being accomplished. To the eyes of men the cross seemed to be the contradiction of every claim that Jesus had ever made concerning God. He had taught them that faith as small as a grain of mustard seed has in it power to move mountains. His rebuke of the legalistic religion of his contemporaries had been that it added to men's burdens instead of opening to them the infinite resources of health and strength that were available in God. The very confidence in God that was reflected in his every word and action was to men a claim upon God's presence and protection. But when his own disciple betrayed him and the authorities conspired to bring his brief mission to a sudden end, where then was God? Observers at the crucifixion are reported to have mocked him, " If you are the Son of God, come down from the cross." For many of his countrymen his death set decisively at rest any suspicion they had harbored that he might be the Messiah of God. God in his omnipotence could not let his Messiah die a shameful death. They might have thought differently had they pondered the words of Second Isaiah, nearly six hundred years earlier, concerning what it costs to serve God's truth in a blind and rebellious world. " It pleased the Lord to bruise his servant " (Isa., ch. 53), because through his Servant's sufferings and death in obedience to the truth he was able to strike from men their blindness and bring his cause to victory. In Gethsemane in lonely struggle Jesus settled with himself the

issue of the meaning of his death. It was the final agoniz-
ing step he had to take in his obedience to the truth of
God. How his death, with his mission hardly more than
started, could be the finishing of his service of God may
have been a mystery even to him. The sweat and tears of
Gethsemane are evidence that he could not face the cross
until he had found meaning in it, a will of God that would
make his death not the negation but the climactic fulfillment of the purpose of his life.

We do not often stop to think how strange it is that
the cross should be the central symbol of the Christian
faith or that in the four Gospels the spotlight of interest
should be so concentrated upon the story of Jesus' death,
or that the church should from the beginning have cele-
brated his death as his triumph. His cross has been his
pulpit across the centuries, from which he has continued
to proclaim his gospel, guarding God's truth from error
by his sacrificial death and breaking down the barriers
with which men defend themselves against it. We must
see two levels of meaning, then, in this one historical event.
We can describe the various factors that converged to send
Jesus to his death and explain it in purely human terms.
He brought it on himself by his intransigent revolt against
the established order of religion in his time. The religious
authorities, fearing his influence, were anxious to be rid
of him, and to the Roman government he was just another
possible instigator of a troublesome popular uprising.
What need of God, then, to explain this event in history?
The historian has told us what happened. But there is another level of meaning to this event, and to all events,
with which the historian does not concern himself, the
level as in Gethsemane where a man asks, " What is
God doing with me in this event? " The event may have
one meaning on the surface, the character of an accident,
or of a judicial murder, or of a national disaster, but a
very different meaning when one wrestles with the question, " What place has this event in the unfolding of God's

purpose for my life? " The final meaning of every event
rests with God and not with men or chance. That is God's
omnipotence, not that he determines what will happen before it happens, but that he and he alone determines ultimately the meaning of whatever happens.

But when we say that the will of God is hidden in every
event, to be revealed to faith, what else is this than God
with man in the midst of his history? *God with man in
the event is " life," even though the event be a death or a
disaster.* However, man without God in the midst of life's
events is man without meaning in his history, man in the
midst of chaos. To Israel in the days of its national disruption the world seemed to have lost all meaning, but
there was a prophet who heard God saying, " God himself who formed the earth . . . did not create it to be a
chaos " (Isa. 45:18). The story of Creation in Gen.,
ch. 1, says this graphically in representing God as bringing an orderly world out of chaos. Emptiness, nothingness,
meaninglessness, chaos, are the enemies of God and man
which through all time threaten God's work and tempt
man to despair. The fear beneath all other fears is that in
the end the events and experiences of life will add up to
nothing and have no destination. Predestination asserts
that there is a purpose of God for each of our lives and for
history as a whole and that nothing can ever happen to
us that has not hidden in it some fragment of that purpose, so that, when it is met with a faith that is an openness to God and to the future that he destines for us, it
carries us one step nearer to our goal.

15

Freedom

NOWHERE DOES OUR PROBLEM of language appear more sharply than with the word " freedom." Round this word cluster the aspirations of humanity, and it has power to set whole continents aflame with revolution. " Freedom Now " is the slogan of American Negroes who have been denied an equal opportunity with their fellow citizens, and in a land that calls itself the home of freedom who can resist their claim? When an oppressive Nazism threatened to overrun the world, " freedom " was the word that made Britons fight on even when their cause seemed hopeless, and when American participation turned the tide of battle, it was in defense of " the four freedoms." Freedom and life are inseparable in our minds. Life without freedom is a poor, mutilated half existence. And yet, when we come to say what freedom is, the definitions go in quite opposite directions. The one that has perhaps the widest popularity and influence defines it as the ability or right of each person to do what he likes with his own life and with everything that is his own without let or hindrance from any quarter. But for any thoughtful person, that is a recipe for anarchy, and for the Christian it defines the very essence of sin. Every man a sovereign, claiming as his right the freedom to do as he likes, makes every man potentially the enemy of every other man and the enemy of any kind of ordered life. But it also pits the human will against the will of God, asserting a freedom for the human self so absolute that the existence or nonexistence of God becomes irrelevant.

In Israel from the very beginning freedom was the gift of God to his people rather than something that Israelites claimed as their natural right. They were slaves in Egypt, but it was not the will of God that they should perish under the oppression of the Egyptians. In his love for them he sent Moses to deliver them and to open the way for them to become a nation in a land of their own. But an all-important step in that deliverance into freedom was Moses' giving of the law. The law defined for Israel the life of freedom. The source of their freedom was in their personal covenant relationship with God. It was before all else a freedom to respond in undivided loyalty and love to God, both in worship and in life. To worship other gods or to degrade their own true God into an idol would be to enslave themselves afresh. The uniqueness of Israel's God was that he alone, in claiming from men their total allegiance, made them not slaves but free men. But they could not be free for him without also being free for the brother alongside them. They had to be custodians of the freedom of the neighbor, and the law spelled out the details of that responsibility: respect for his life, for his family, and for his possessions.

This tradition that freedom was intrinsic to the covenant relationship with God had a powerful influence upon the shaping of Israelite character. It created an atmosphere that made tyranny an alien thing rather than the normal form of political order as in other Eastern lands. The authority of the earthly king was conditioned by the authority of Israel's unseen king to whom every knee, of king and commoner alike, must bow. The law of God took precedence over every man-made law. Therefore, the humblest Israelite had rights which not even the most powerful king could ignore, and the prophet of God made himself in each successive age the spokesman of the poor who were being defrauded of their freedom.

Freedom 109

At first sight the New Testament seems to concern itself with the liberation of men from bondages within themselves, from sicknesses of body and spirit, rather than from social and political forms of oppression. Jesus is sent to save his people from their sins. His attention seems focused more upon what men are doing to enslave themselves than upon their exploitation by others. When Paul speaks of " the freedom wherewith Christ hath made you free," this is a freedom of man in the service of God, which is being contrasted with the narrow and restricted existence that a man has in the confines of a legalistic religion. It is the " freedom of the sons of God " who as " new men in Christ " are being emancipated from " the world of sin and death." This difference of focus in the New Testament has in some quarters been made an excuse for ignoring the prophetic tradition with its passionate advocacy of the underdog and its courageous exposure of injustice and oppression and for asserting that Jesus and the New Testament church had no interest in social and political problems but only in saving men's souls from sin. Christian freedom is therefore defined as an inner spiritual freedom which is unrelated to the issues that arise in the social, political, and economic life of the community. There were earnestly pious people in the Nazi period in Germany who were content to enjoy their " spiritual " freedom without asking any questions about whether or not a Christian should be free to obey Jesus Christ in his political decisions and in his relations with his fellow citizens of a non-Aryan race.

At such a point as this the Old Testament becomes an invaluable guardian of Christian truth. To tear Jesus and Paul out of their context in continuity with the prophets of Israel is to pervert their significance. For Jesus as for the prophets there could be no separation between the inner and the outer life. He too was the spokesman of those who were suffering and neglected because of the blindness and callousness of their neighbors. In his picturing of the

Last Judgment (Matt., ch. 25), it is not men's professions of faith that count but how they have responded to the need of the hungry, the homeless, and the prisoner. Asked to define a neighbor, he quickly sketches a scene on the road from Jerusalem to Jericho, with a man lying naked and bleeding at the roadside where robbers had left him. To represent Jesus as unconcerned about social problems such as poverty, race, and injustice is a monstrosity. Why then the difference in his approach? We get a clue to the answer in the account of his temptations. The hunger of men for bread claimed his deep concern, so deep that he was tempted to spend his life in the attempt to satisfy it, but more urgent than the need for bread was the need of men to feed upon the word of God. Beneath the social and economic evils that left men without their daily bread was the starvation of men's selves for lack of God. They were inhuman with one another because they were no longer open to the source of their humanity in God. First and foremost, then, with Jesus was the task of shattering men's self-engrossment, which frequently was a religious self-engrossment, and of laying them open both to God and to their fellowmen. He set them free to live by speaking to them, and being to them, the word in which God claims for himself his rightful place at the center of man's life and by his presence excludes the fear, anxiety, hatred, pride, and all the other passions that enslave a man within himself and make him the oppressor of his fellowman.

The paradox of Christian freedom stands out sharply in the person of Jesus. He is the slave of God, his will molded into one with the will of God himself, his love for his fellowman the infinitely forgiving love of God, his life completely at the service of God's purpose in the world. And yet for him to be completely bound to God was to be completely free. For God to be the absolute sovereign in his human existence resulted not in any slavishness but in perfect freedom. One can speak of a sovereign freedom of Jesus, a freedom in the truth, the freedom of a king, whose kingliness is nowhere more evident than when he stands before his accusers and his judges and when he hangs upon his cross. His freedom was the gift of God, and no man could take it from him. He was free because God by his nature cannot be enslaved to anyone or anything, and to have one's life in God, that is, in openness and response to God, reflecting in a human life the very nature of God, is to be made a sharer in God's freedom. Therefore, when Jesus offers to share with us his life in God, it means letting ourselves be bound to God as he was bound and discovering that, far from being a form of bondage, this binding is our liberation from every form of bondage into the freedom of the sons of God.

A Christian, then, is free not by permission of his government but by the grace of God. The very nature of his life in God demands of him that he think and act in freedom. Freedom is intrinsic to a truly human life. But if that is so, a Christian cannot be content to have this freedom for himself while men all about him in the world are still without it. He thinks and speaks and acts in freedom, refusing to be coerced by pressures of any kind, but what he claims for himself he has also to claim for his fellowman. He is the enemy of every form of enslavement and oppression that men inflict upon their fellowmen.

Perhaps now we begin to see more clearly the sharp distinction between Christian freedom that is God's gift to man in a personal relationship with himself and a freedom that each man claims for himself as a natural right, even though he may recognize limitations which must be placed upon it for the protection of his neighbors. The first is by its nature disciplined and responsible freedom, freedom *for* God and *for* the neighbor, whereas the other is freedom for oneself, if necessary *from* God and *from* the neighbor. The first, because it is inseparable from the binding of man to God, cannot be surrendered without the surrender of our life in God, but the other is negotiable since it has no deeper rootage than the self-interest of man.

When Nazi totalitarianism attained a power in Europe against which there seemed to be no longer any practicable resistance, many men who formerly had seemed to be the spokesmen for human freedom now in self-interest counseled submission. It was still within their choice how much freedom of speech and action to claim for themselves and for others. But there were other men and women for whom there was no such choice. They were bound to a Lord who bestowed on them a freedom that was not negotiable. And Nazi totalitarianism found in these free Christians a wall of resistance which it could not break.

Freedom is the atmosphere that the human self requires to breathe. Its forms are legion and its enemies are legion. Freedom to choose, to think, to act, is essential to the growth of character in a child, and the enemy is the parent who, consciously or unconsciously, dictates the choices, thoughts, and actions. Freedom of the mind to follow wherever the facts may seem to lead, no matter what existing interests may be threatened by the conclusions, is essential to the sciences, and when an authoritarian government or church or social class attempts to control the findings of its scholars, it becomes an enemy of freedom, truth, and God. Freedom of opportunity regardless of race, class, or color is essential to the peace of society, for its denial is felt to be a form of slavery and generates hostility which can destroy the society itself. Yet one race or class or color can become so complacent in the enjoyment of its superior opportunities that it fails to detect the explosive passions on its borders. Freedom of prophecy is required if the Christian pulpit is to perform its function, declaring in season and out a word from God to his people, exposing them continually to both his judgment and his mercy. And when subtle, or not so subtle, pressures are allowed to dull the edges of the two-edged sword that is the word of God, it were far, far better and more honest for the church to close its doors.

The threat to freedom comes often from an unexpected

quarter, and the church as the guardian of man's freedom should be alert to detect and warn of its approach. Hitler diverted attention from what he himself was doing to strip men of their freedoms by keeping their eyes fixed on the terrors of Communism on the horizon. So also today, a nation preoccupied with resisting Communism in Asia and Europe is in danger of remaining unaware of the gradual disappearance of freedoms at home. There is no Hitler or Stalin to tyrannize over us, but there is a colossal expansion of the power of government, an ever closer meshing of vast corporations with the institutions of government and in particular with the military authorities, and a careful control and slanting of the information that reaches the public, which together constitute a serious threat to a free citizenry. Mind control is not a device employed only by the evil Fascists and Communists. The multiple channels of modern communication constantly bombard us with propaganda skillfully designed to make us think in conformity with the policies of " big brother who knows what is best for us." Freedom of thought, freedom of decision, and freedom of speech become ever more difficult to sustain, and only a perpetual vigilance and determined search for dependable information make possible an intelligent and humane approach to the problems of today.

Christians should be shocked awake by the way in which, during the Vietnam war, a policy of escalation has been pursued in spite of the protests of a large section of the nation, the almost unanimous opposition of the Christian churches and the faculties and students of the universities, and the appeals of nations that we would expect to be allied with us in any international conflict. But Vietnam is only one decision. There will be others, and what must be grasped now is that the will of thoughtful and humane citizens will be disregarded again and again unless the present concentration of power in the hands of a small circle of men can somehow be counteracted and the men made responsible to the public for their policies and

actions. We have long been scornful of the way in which
freedom has been a casualty to the " system " in communist lands but unconscious of the development of a
" system " in our own supposedly democratic society which
by more subtle means exerts its pressures upon the citizen.
Financial security, success in one's vocation, and general
social acceptability may sometimes seem more important
than freedom to think for oneself and to speak with integrity. Every minister of a Christian church knows that
temptation, and so also do millions of employees and ex-
ecutives in the business world. The front line in the battle
for man's freedom to be human is not far across the sea
but cuts directly through every place of business, every
community, every home, every church, and if we know our
own souls, through the existence of every living person.
And the loss of freedom is death.

16

Truth

WHEN THE AUTHOR of the Fourth Gospel defined truth
as a person, or perhaps we should say as the life and
light that were incarnate in a person, little did he know
that he was preparing the way for the church of the twentieth century to face and master one of the most difficult
and critical problems in its history. The church stands or
falls by the truth of its gospel. But not always has it let
itself be guided by the Fourth Gospel in its definition of
the truth. The idea has long been rooted in the mind of
Western man that truth is strictly an affair of the intellect.
Man's reason has been given to him to ferret out the truth
in every realm of life, and then, when once he knows the
truth, he can decide what to do about it. Of course, it
had to be recognized that the truths of faith were not directly available to the intellect of any man but had to be
revealed, as was the Messiahship of Jesus to Peter at
Caesarea Philippi. Once revealed, however, they were regarded in much the same way as all other truths, as concepts to be affirmed by the mind. Truth and life, truth and
being, truth and action, were separated from each other.
The truths of the Christian faith could then be set forth in
a series of affirmations to be weighed by the mind. Faith
was defined as the acceptance of these affirmations. First,
a person had to be convinced that the affirmations were
true, and then he could go on to a second stage where he
would ask himself what he must do and what kind of life

he must live on the basis of these truths.

The tenacity of this approach to Christian truth is due to the fact that this is how we operate in so many other areas of life. The truth that a judge and jury try to determine is a purely intellectual affair. Personal considerations must be excluded from the courtroom. The task is to ascertain the facts of the case as accurately as possible and then on the basis of the facts to decide what should be done. The truth for the scientist with his microscope and test tube is available to him no matter what kind of man he is; his mind can operate in almost complete detachment from his personal relationships. The truth for the historian has until recently been taken to be wholly a reproduction of what actually happened at a certain time and place, objective facts to be searched out by rational investigation. Moreover, this concept of truth has in these realms proved itself valid, and the activities based upon it have made most impressive contributions to human welfare. It is not surprising that men expect the concept to remain valid universally. But when man's person and personal relationships are the subject of knowledge, it begins to lose some, though certainly not all, of its validity. Physiology, psychology, anthropology, and the social sciences have been able as sciences to bring to light a factual knowledge about man which has liberated us from past ignorance and misconceptions, has widened and deepened our understanding of ourselves, and has thus prepared the way for more intelligent attitudes and actions. But because in these sciences man looks at man and has no other vantage point from which to look except his own existence in a network of human relationships, the truths arrived at always reflect to some degree the personal stance of the investigator, especially when they involve assumptions concerning the nature and destiny of man. The scientist here begins to find it difficult to keep truth and life apart. This at least should be sufficient to suggest that in a realm where we are concerned not just with truths about man and his relationships but with the truth of man's existence in his relationship with God, with his fellowman, and with himself, a different concept of truth may be in order.

In the New Testament truth and life are inseparable. There is no knowledge of the truth without the whole of life being involved. To know the truth is to know God and in knowing God to know oneself in a wholly new way. To know God is not a possibility for any mind in detachment from life because to know God is to stand before him as we are, in a personal relationship in which we are far more conscious of being known than of knowing. Truth here is not a special set of facts concerning God and man which can be observed and affirmed in intellectual detachment; truth is the reality of the relationships in which we have our existence.

What, then, does it mean to call Jesus Christ " the Truth " and to expect to know the truth in knowing him? It is an affirmation that in him the true life of man with God and with his fellowman has been revealed in being lived out in the midst of men. At this one point in history and in this one person the meaning of God, the meaning of man's life, the meaning of history, and the meaning of the world are disclosed, not primarily as truths which can be set down in propositions, but as a life in Jesus Christ in which God is with man, a life that through him can become the life of every man. The truth of God and the life of man in God are one. Therefore this truth cannot be known by even the most brilliant intellect in separation from the life. The life is the concrete expression of the truth.

Truth in the Old Testament is of the same nature. The prophets are men who speak the truth without fear or favor of any man. They speak only what God gives them to speak. Only false prophets have freedom to temper their message to make it congenial to their hearers. Absolute integrity is the mark of the true prophet, and it gives to his work such priceless worth that the prophets of Israel can never cease to speak to men. But what is this truth which is the burden of their sermons to Israel? They strip away the illusions of their fellow citizens concerning themselves and their relationship with God and face them with the reality of what they are, but they have eyes to do this only because they constantly see the community in the light of God's intention for it and God's relation to it. Truth and life for them are one and have their existence in the personal covenant relationship of God with man. To know the truth is to know one's existence imperiled by the brokenness of the relation and at the same time to know the possibility and the promise of its healing through the mercy and faithfulness of God.

This, then, is the truth that has been entrusted to the church to make known to all men, a truth that no one ever rightly knows until it is his life, but, mark you, a truth that is present and available to be known wherever the life and light that were incarnate in Jesus Christ have become through him a life and light in other men! The truth of the Christian gospel cannot be communicated to a world that is in confusion and agony for lack of it merely through preaching, teaching, and Sacraments; the life of freedom in the truth that was the life of Jesus Christ has to become the life of a community of men now if the truth entrusted to them is to shine as a light in the world. And if the life of those who call themselves the Christian church is in contradiction to the life revealed in Christ, no amount of passionate affirmation of the truth in preaching and teaching can overcome the distrust engendered by the contradiction.

The church has in the past only too often confused itself, its members, and men in general by a failure to hold fast to the Biblical understanding of truth. Confessions made in all the earnestness of a faith that stands its ground against error have been interpreted as though they were final and infallible statements of divine truth, now to be guarded jealously by the church against any change, faith being equated with the acceptance of the statements as true and any questioning of them in any detail being branded as a deadly sin. It is not so long since such questioning could be punishable by death. An even more widespread and paralyzing error has been the indiscriminate identification of the contents of the Bible with the truth to which the Christian must give unquestioning assent. Three centuries ago a Roman Catholic scholar studying the early chapters of Genesis was puzzled about where Cain could find a wife if he and his parents were the sole inhabitants of the earth. He concluded that there must have been other people on earth in addition to those mentioned in the Bible and he published his conclusion. Very quickly he found himself in jail for questioning the truth of Scripture and remained there until he recanted. At that time Catholic and Protestant churches and the Jewish synagogues were alike agreed that jail was the proper punishment for such questioners. Much closer to our own time scholars whose one aim in life was to understand the Scriptures better by applying to them the methods of literary and historical investigation which are universally accepted in the modern world have had to suffer persecution and deprivation at the hands of their fellow Christians for whom the text of Scripture was from end to end infallible truth. It is so pathetic that in the Roman Church, in spite of all the recent advances, the defense of truth is still to some degree the defense of a series of infallible dogmas such as the infallibility of the head of the Roman Church or the assumption of the Virgin Mary, and that so widely in the Protestant Church the defense of truth is the defense of every narrative in Scripture as an inerrant report of exactly what happened once upon a time. It is pathetic because both positions are so vulnerable and indefensible and because they both distract the minds of men from the truth that is life, the life of God with man, to which the whole of Scripture witnesses, and which asks not to be defended but to be let loose among men to overthrow their enemies and to make of them new men.

Only this Biblical understanding of truth can survive the relativizing of everything human, which is one of the consequences of modern historical research. To be human is to exist in a historical context and to be conditioned by that context. To be human is to be constantly becoming. The world refuses to stand still, and in the modern age the pace of change has so accelerated that we are much more conscious of the movement than ever men were before. Once, men were inclined to think that the truths they had discovered in physics or in medicine or in history would remain true forever, but there are few " truths " of 1867 in these regions that have not had to be radically revised or abandoned by 1967. The advance of knowledge now is such that after ten years out of college the doctor or the engineer who has not kept abreast of the advances of his science is hopelessly and dangerously out of date. But change did not begin yesterday. The historian unfolds to us the millennia of change that are the story of how man has become what now he is. He has often been tempted along the way to try to stop the process, to hold the world still, at a point where life seemed to him to have reached a satisfactory concretion. But always there has come a shaking and a dissolution of the static order prized by man, and he has been forced to make his way into a new and unanticipated world. Whatever answers he had to life's problems in the past, he has had to think his way through all of them again. Everything human is subject to change. It is the nature of man's life in history that he is on his way toward an unseen goal and he cannot stop more than a moment anywhere along the way.

The illusion still persists in the minds of many Christians that somehow in everything that pertains to their faith they are exempted from this restless process of historical change. But the prophets and the apostles found their point of absolute stability not in anything human but in the word of God in which God manifests his presence

with man afresh in every age. The New Testament itself
exhibits forcefully the marks of human change. The gospel
that Jesus preached was expressed in the language and
thought forms of the Jewish world in which he lived, but
when that gospel began to be preached beyond the Jewish world to Greeks and Romans, a different language and
quite different thought forms had to be called into play.
Because the truth was not condensed in propositions, but
was incarnate in a personal life and had its primary existence in persons rather than in a book, there was in it
a mobility, a capacity to find expression in new ways in
each new situation and in each new culture. The history
of the church and of theology is a convincing demonstration of the relativity of everything human and Christians,
when they have thought themselves to have escaped from
the relativity of history into a state of final and absolute
truth, they have merely anchored themselves to the broken
lights of an era that is past. God does not need infallible
men in order to get his work done in the world; he needs
only faithful and obedient, courageously obedient, men. In
fact, infallible men are always self-righteous men and deluded men since they think themselves to be in complete
possession of the truth. If the New Testament teaches us
anything, it is this: All men are sinful and fallible and not
even the Spirit of God is able to make humble servants
of the truth of self-righteous men who deny their fallibility.
We have to be content like Paul to see through a glass
darkly and never to forget the brokenness of our relation
to the truth we serve, a brokenness that has daily to be
mended by God's grace and our repentance.

One final word. To have one's life rooted and grounded
in this personal truth of God makes one open to truth
from whatever quarter it may come and unafraid to face
any problems that arise in the understanding either of
Scripture or of the doctrines of the church. The truth of
God cannot ultimately be in contradiction to any truth.
Indeed, the devotion of scholars in the pursuit of truth in

literature, history, and the sciences has often forced Christians to rethink their understanding of the truth of God and to abandon untenable positions. But when Christians are asked to break their continuity with the truth and life to which the prophets and apostles bear their witness in order to keep abreast of what are acclaimed as the truths of modern man, the time is then arrived to turn upon these " truths " the same searching critique to which we have exposed our own most cherished " truths."

17

Love

PAUL, in what is perhaps the most well-known passage in all his writings (I Cor., ch. 13), makes love the *sine qua non* of a Christian faith. Let a man have all the gifts of the Spirit except this, let him be ever so eloquent in Christian speech, let him be an accomplished theologian, let him have such faith that he would willingly die for the gospel or such generosity that he would give all his possessions to the poor, but if he has no love, it all counts for nothing and he is no Christian. It is evident that for Paul love is not just one quality in a Christian's character or one element in his attitude toward his fellowmen. Rather, it is the central core of a Christian's existence which determines the quality and character of everything else. His oratory is empty, his theology is intellectual gymnastics, his charities are exhibitionist, and even his martyrdom is wasted unless at the center of his being he has been mastered and possessed by the kind of love that broke in upon the life of man in the person of Jesus Christ. " Love " is the word that Paul used to describe the life, the new humanity, the true humanity, the life in God, that in Jesus Christ was born into the world and was no less than the dawning of a new age. Love is the mark of the new age. Therefore a church that has oratory, theological wisdom, generous charities, and even martyrs but whose members are not indwelt and shaped in all their attitudes by God's love is still essentially mired in the old age of sin and death and has not yet begun to live in the new age inaugurated by Jesus Christ.

The word " love " is used so loosely and with so many shades of meaning in common speech today that one has to penetrate a fog screen to reach the Christian meaning of the word. It can express a taste for candy, " I love chocolates," or the vagaries of passion. Most people would classify it as an emotion, and to them it would be inconceivable that anyone should love without emotion. They identify love itself so directly with the feeling they experience that the absence of the feeling is to them the absence of love. There is no more fertile source of disruption in marriage today than this inability to distinguish between the reality of love and the feeling of love. Christian marriage is founded not primarily on a feeling or an emotion but on a relation, a covenantal bond in which two people have committed themselves to each other before God to hold to each other through all the changing weather of their human feelings. Love, in the Christian understanding of it, is primarily a relation before it is a feeling.

How true this is appears at once when we examine the uses of the word " love " in the New Testament. When Jesus undertook to express in a parable the love of neighbor, he chose two men who would have no reason to feel even friendly toward each other. Samaritans were detested by Jews. But when the Samaritan found a Jew lying naked and bleeding at the roadside, he interrupted his journey to care for the man in his need and to provide for his recovery. Love was compassion for a fellow human being in his hour of need. How the Samaritan as a Samaritan felt toward a Jew as a Jew was of no significance when the Jew as a neighbor was in need. So also when Jesus issues his new command to his disciples, " Love your enemies " (we need to remember that he and his disciples had bitter enemies in the Palestinian community, enemies who would stop at nothing to silence what seemed to them subversive teaching), he was not asking the disciples to conjure up a feeling of love toward their enemies, but rather to let their relation to them be one of openness, care, and understanding, and not one of antagonism. It has sometimes been pointed out that Jesus' condemnations of his enemies, the Pharisees, were not exactly loving, but this criticism assumes that where one loves one could never be so sharply critical. On the contrary, love that is openness, care, and understanding of the fellowman may have to use words that cut deeply and offend in order to deal honestly with him. " Speaking the truth in love " was one of the salient characteristics of the Christian fellowship in its earliest stages, for the love which the disciples had learned at close quarters from Jesus Christ was not a gentle kindliness in human relations that shrank from any word that might offend but rather a care for the brother that had the courage to risk offending him if there was truth he needed to be told. It is not so much what we *feel* but what we *are* toward our fellowman that determines in the Christian sense whether or not we love.

Another source of misunderstanding is the false antithesis that is sometimes posed between the Old Testament as law and the New as love. It is a grave injustice to the Hebrews and a crude misreading of the Old Testament. The whole of life in the Old Testament is rooted and grounded in the love of God. The covenant relation between God and Israel has its source in his loving choice of Israel to be a people in his service and in fellowship with him, and what the covenant relation claims of Israel is a love in response to God's love that will compass totally the existence of the nation. But the love of God is not for Israel alone. God's choice of Israel is that through Israel he may reach out to the ends of the earth and draw all mankind into covenant with himself. God's love for man and for the world is the secret of all his actions. His wrath at man's sin and disobedience does not contradict his love but must be understood as the obverse of it; God is not willing that man in his blindness should destroy himself. The painfulness of sin which man experiences as the wrath of God is the severity of God's love that sets obstacles in the path of prodigal man in order to turn him from the way of death to the way of life. Thus, in the Old Testament the personal relation between God and man is always primary. The prophets' appeal is not " Keep the law and all will be well " but " Return unto the Lord your God who loves you." Love is meaningless, however, without obedience, and the commandments spell out in terms of obedience the character of a people's life which is being lived in loving response to God. Again, it is here evident that the word " love " describes a relation rather than a feeling. How Israel felt about God was quite secondary to how the nation responded to him in the concrete situations and actions of its life.

If love is so central to the Old Testament, one may be inclined to ask what remained for Jesus to add. What is new about love in the New Testament? First, we need to realize that in Judaism the priority of love to law had been lost from sight. The covenant relation had become more legal than personal. God's love was reserved for those who kept the law. Jesus cut through this narrowness and legalism to reclaim the prophetic gospel of the Old Testament in which the love of God for Israel called forth an answering love in man. But he went far beyond the prophets. The prophets proclaimed the loving care of God for Israel and called men to return and find their life in God. But in Jesus the love of God went in search of men. The father in Jesus' parable, running down the road to meet the returning prodigal and embracing him with a generosity of love that overflows all bounds, unveils to us the very heart of Jesus' understanding of God. And that representation of the Father's love was sketched by him in defense of his own love toward prodigals! God's love does not wait for men to repent and return to him; it goes in search of them. The difference between Old and New Testament is evident in a comparison of John the Baptist and Jesus. John waited at the Jordan River for the people to come to him and in response to his message to register their repentance and their determination to lead a new life. In contrast to this, Jesus went in search of the men and women who needed him. He sought them in the synagogues, in the streets, in their homes, and from one town to another. He enlisted disciples to speed and extend the search. His mission was in haste because it was intolerable that any man should be left ignorant of the life that was awaiting him in the loving care of God.

The heart of Jesus' mission and of his gospel, then, was the *incarnation* of divine love. In him the love of God came out of the distant heavens, and while still remaining the infinite compassion of God, became a love that spoke with a human voice and reached out to men with human hands. This was what men had not known before, not even the prophets of Israel, that God can so indwell a human person that that person becomes a bridge from God to other men. Through the centuries men had sought and found forgiveness in God, and it had seemed that God had to wait for men to seek him. But now the forgiveness of God walked the earth in search of men. Forgiveness as it met men in Jesus was the love of God in action, invading a world that was in captivity to sin to set men free for their true life in fellowship with him and with one another. God has two ways of battling evil in the life of mankind. One is the way of discipline, to make the evil so painful in its consequences that men will turn from it in fear, which only restrains the evil and does not overcome it. But his other better way is to forgive the sin, which is not an overlooking of it but a personal dealing with it, a love and mercy in whose presence the sinner hates the sin that has robbed him of his life in God, so that the sin begins to be torn up by its roots. Forgiveness is the weapon with which God abolishes sin. Jesus' mission was a wielding of that weapon with tremendous power, and when he chose disciples to share his mission with him, he expected them to meet men with the same forgiveness and to extend his conquests.

But it had to be the same forgiveness. There is another kind of forgiveness that men practice, a limited forgiveness that has no power in it to accomplish anything. Peter was familiar with it when he inquired of Jesus whether it was sufficient to forgive his brother seven times. He was impatient to be done forgiving. His forgiveness was little more than a restraining of retaliation. It had in it nothing of the infinite and unfailing love of God. " Not seven times, but seventy times seven," Jesus said to Peter. And this is the amazing expectation that Jesus had of Peter and has of everyone who would count himself his disciple: He should forgive as God forgives, not with a grudging, calculating spirit, but with a generosity like God's generosity, caring only as God cares, that men should be liberated from the evils and offenses that obstruct their lives.

For " Peter " read " church." The church was called into being by Jesus to be a community of disciples in whom God's love would continue to invade the world. But before it could invade the world, the love had first to master and possess the disciple. And to be mastered and possessed by the love of God was to be mastered and possessed by God. God's love is not detachable from God. Therefore, for men to love as God loves and to forgive as God forgives was for them to be centered no longer in self but in God. The old self had to die and a new self be born, one that would respond to God with a love that would be a reflection of God's own love. This was the life of the new covenant initiated by Jesus, a life of man in God and of God in man, of man with God and God with man, which opened a whole new future before humanity. Even in deeply committed disciples, though, the new age met with obstacles. The old self dies hard. In Judas the old blind self refused to die and preferred to send Jesus to his death! To Peter it was not only an infinite forgiveness that seemed at first unreasonable; he was deeply puzzled that there was not a simpler and less costly way to redeem mankind. The church has been looking for less costly strategies ever since, and it constantly underestimates the resistance of the human self. Jesus knew the tenacity of the old self, the slowness with which men's eyes open to the truth and their hearts open to the love of God. The only answer to the problem was for him simply to be what he was, a man in whom, because he was at one with God, the love and truth of God confronted men and forced them to stand either with God or against him. He paid the cost of being what he was upon his cross, which thus becomes the symbol of the resistance of the human self to God and at the same time the mark of how far the love of God will go to win its battle. The cross dictates to the church the strategy in the ongoing battle with man's sin and blindness. We can take no other road than first was taken. The cross marks out the road by which God's love invades the world. There has to be a people so bound to Christ by the love with which he has redeemed them from themselves that they have no other life than the life they have from him, a life in God that is like his life in God, so ruled by God's love for man that it refuses to be turned from its purpose by any obstacle or threat.

Too often what passes as love within the Christian fellowship is little more than mutuality, a friendliness of like-minded people for one another. " I will love you if you will love me." The fragility of such love is evident in the speed with which it vanishes should there be any serious difference of opinion or any giving of offense. Jesus was scornful of the people who loved and showed kindness only where they could expect love and kindness in return. That was essentially a self-centered rather than a God-centered love. It belonged to the old age of self-centeredness and death rather than to the new age of God-centeredness and life. The only love with power to redeem men out of death into life was a love like God's love that gave itself where it was not deserved, that poured itself out where it could count on no response, that loved the enemy in order to overcome in men that which made them enemies of God and of themselves. Mutuality masquerading as Christian love creates a church turned inward on itself and irrelevant in relation to the world that waits to be redeemed. But the love of God is for the world that does not even know its need, and when his love begins to take possession of the church, it turns it outward to the world and lays that world upon its heart so that in its every part its one concern is how best it can serve God's purpose to bring life to every man.

18

Peace

" AND ON EARTH PEACE." The song of the angels is sung
by millions of Christians around the earth each Christmas-
time. But they do not any longer expect real peace, the end
of war, the cessation of destructive conflicts. A cease-fire
in the current Vietnam war, with time for the soldiers to
have turkey with cranberry sauce and plum pudding for
dinner, and for the folks at home to have a day with a
minimum of war news! In our kind of world is that all one
can expect? Surely the early Christians were not so dreamy
as to think the coming of Christ would stop the nations
from fighting! The modern Christian knows, or thinks he
knows, the impossibility of that and shifts his focus from
peace on earth to peace of mind. He pins a wavering hope
on the United Nations to discourage wars and disassociates
his Christian faith from problems of world peace.

But a Christian who takes the Biblical basis and character of his faith seriously cannot so easily free his Christ
from involvement in international conflicts. First consider
the Old Testament hope that Jesus Christ fulfilled. The
psalmist in the midst of world-shaking events put his trust
in a God who would one day break the bows of men and
burn their chariots in the fire, making wars to cease unto
the ends of the earth. The prophet saw a day coming when
all mankind in obedience to the command of God would
abandon the arts of war and would refashion their arma-
ments into instruments of peace. Even the wolf, the lion,

and the serpent would become as harmless as a lamb, and
neither man nor beast would any longer do each other
harm. It was inconceivable to the Old Testament faith that
a God who cared for man and his world should will the
conflicts that brought such loss and sorrow to whole nations. They were a brutal contradiction of his will for
man, and to believe in his sovereignty in history was to believe that one day his gracious purpose for his creation
must triumph.

The Kingdom of God which was the burden of Jesus'
preaching was nothing less than the sovereignty of God in
his creation, not sovereignty in a distant heaven or at some
future date when God would suddenly transform all things,
but sovereignty now. The good news of the gospel was that
men did not have to wait any longer for God's great new
world to dawn; it was open to them in the very moment in
which they were living if only they would be open to it.
The word they heard in Jesus' preaching and teaching was
the seed of the Kingdom. In it God himself, the sovereign
God, was present, hiddenly working his will. To receive
the seed into the soil of one's life was to receive the sovereign God himself, and to respond to him in faith and obedience was to begin already to be sons of his Kingdom.
Jesus saw his Kingdom coming in the transformation of
men's lives through the hearing of his gospel and the receiving of his forgiveness. When his disciples on their first
mission brought healing to men's bodies and liberation
from evil spirits, he exclaimed with joy that through their
ministry God was winning fresh victories over the powers
of evil. When he taught them to pray, " Thy kingdom
come, thy will be done, *on earth* as it is in heaven," he
did not intend them to have their eyes and their hopes set
on some distant day at the end of time but on the present.
He might well have said, " Thy kingdom come *now* on
earth."

It is equally clear that for Jesus the coming of the Kingdom was the coming of peace. The ultimate consequences

of God's sovereignty might be hidden for the present, but they would not always remain hidden. The Kingdom would not be the Kingdom if it did not make an end of every vicious conflict. The forgiveness of God freed men of the sin that alienated them not only from God but from themselves, an alienation that as long as it lasts is the source of ever new disturbances in human relations. To be forgiven by God is to be taught a spirit of forgiveness that cancels out and overcomes the offenses of other men. This new openness to God and confidence in the love of God brought freedom also from the anxiety about things that darkens each day with fear for so many people. To think and act in fear is the antithesis of thinking and acting in faith. Fear blinds men so that they no longer know what they are doing, and what seems to them to be merely self-defense is actually aggression against a fellowman. Fear conjures up enemies on every horizon. But where there is faith in God and openness to his love there can be no fear. To be wholly in the hands of God is to be beyond the reach of any power in heaven or earth to do us harm. We can understand, then, why the early Christians called Jesus " the Prince of Peace." It was not just a formal transfer to him of one of the Old Testament messianic titles. It was their witness to the new order of life which he had brought into being and in which they now had their existence. " Peace on earth " was actuality for them, and they were certain that what was actuality for them was possibility and promise for all mankind.

What then did Jesus mean when he said, " I am come to bring not peace but a sword "? Here we have to speak of paradox. What seem to be contradictory statements are in reality the two halves of a single truth, and, separated, neither one of them is true. It is like Jesus telling us that we have to deny ourselves in order to be our true selves, that we have to die to live. Death and life are opposites to us. To die is the negation of life, but not in the realm where man has to do with God. When we stand before God, we

discover that our life is suspended between two contradictory worlds, an old world in which self is sovereign and a
new world in which infinite new possibilities appear when
the self is humbled before God. An old self and an old
world have to die if the new self and the new world are to
be born. So also here, the Prince of Peace, when he comes
to establish the peace of his new order in the midst of men,
has first of all to meet and overcome the blind resistance
and stubborn antagonism of an old world and an old self
in man. It is always a puzzle to us why Jesus with his gospel of love and forgiveness and with his mission of healing
for the ills of men should have stirred such bitter hatred
and murderous opposition among the most virtuous and
religious people in the community. We are puzzled because we do not ourselves recognize the costliness of the
surrender to God which Jesus claims from men. To let
God's Kingdom come is to let God be really sovereign in
us, which means the abdication of our self-rule. Our virtue and our religiousness no longer justify our pride of self.
We are blind to the realities of our own lives when we
think that the presence of God with man in Jesus Christ
should have been greeted universally with shouts of joy.
The nearness of God is a threat always to the self-sovereignty of man and to the established order in which he has
made himself at home. The coming of God's Kingdom of
peace is always felt as a disturbance, a revolution, a sword
that slays. It would not be God's peace if it did not first
overthrow and conquer the old order of a humanity alienated from God. Jeremiah was saying exactly what Jesus
said when he warned his fellow countrymen that the word
of God which he served was both destructive and constructive. It would destroy, root out, and tear down, and
then it would build and plant a new order in Israel. The
peace promised in the gospel does not come without revolution.

Nowhere today does the pride and self-confidence of
man meet with such frustration as in the attempt to make

peace on earth. We revel in the achievements of science and technology in the Western world, the conquest of disease, the transformation of living conditions for the common man, the inventions which do so much to open up the world to every man, and now the explorations of space. We point with pride to the advances in our social order which protect the workman from exploitation and from poverty in his times of unemployment or in old age. We have applied our science to solve the painful problems which arise from the sickness and disorder of men's personalities. At times we tell ourselves that man has only to extend the development of his sciences to solve all the problems of human life and to create for himself a new world. And then we come down out of the clouds as we open our eyes upon a world that is balanced on the edge of self-annihilation and acknowledge that this too is what we proud citizens of the Western world have brought into being. We seem to have two souls within a single body. With one we are devoted to the interests of humanity, eager to use all our talents and resources to improve the lot of man, but with the other we are savages, ready to use all our ingenuity and our power to kill and destroy when we consider that our interests are in danger. And by contemplating the virtues of the first we give ourselves good consciences and remain confident of our virtue even in our most savage acts of destruction.

Why has Western man, with 1900 years of Christian influence behind him, generated such conflict and destructiveness in the twentieth century? Two world wars within thirty years, sending millions to their deaths and laying waste whole areas of the earth, provoked not by primitive barbarians but by nations which seemed to be at the very summit of civilized life, nations which only a generation ago called themselves " Christian nations "! How was it possible, in the land where the Protestant churches had their birth and so many fruitful movements in Christian thought and life had their origin, for six million of the

Jewish race to be hounded to their deaths merely because
they shared their race with Jesus Christ? But we must
bring the problem closer home. How is it possible for
the American nation, with such a high percentage of its
people members of Christian churches and with its traditional claim to be the encourager and friend of a struggling
humanity everywhere, not only to blunder into a highly
questionable war against a tiny Asiatic people but, in doing so, to risk the outbreak of an atomic war that would
devastate more than half the earth?

It is time that Western Christians faced honestly this
conundrum of their existence. It is our society, this Western world for which we are responsible, which is endanger-
ing the future of humanity. We talk peace, we pray for
peace, we organize for peace, but there is an untamed self
in us that in its self-assertion carries us blindly into conflict on every level of our life. Hitler we regarded as a can-
cerous growth on our civilization for whom we had no responsibility, but Hitler was merely an outrageous magnifi-
cation of the principle of self-sovereignty which everywhere
today expresses itself in aggressive nationalism. Couched
in more urbane and individualistic terms, the same principle forms the core of the philosophy of life which is most
popular in America and which issues in a more blind and
brutal nationalism than is usually acknowledged. We act as
though there were no law in heaven or earth superior to
our national self-interest, but we hide from ourselves the
actual character of our actions by covering them with a
veneer of idealistic altruism. When Russia invaded Hun-
gary in order to guard its western frontier, we called it
" barbarous aggression," but when we invaded Cuba to
guard our southern frontier, we called it " the defense of
democratic freedom." Idealism encourages illusions about
ourselves. We judge ourselves by the nobility of our idealistic intentions, while we judge other nations by their actual performance. Idealism is a philosophy that not only
leaves the self-will of man untamed but provides a rational

justification for his determination to be the center of his world. A gospel that calls on man to die to self in order to find his true self in God falls on deaf ears when the hearers are already committed to a philosophy of self-sovereignty.

Self-sovereignty means eternal conflict of self with self, race with race, class with class, nation with nation. It issues in an order of life for which there can be no peace. Today the principle of self-sovereignty in the white community in America and South Africa is awakening, as is inevitable, a similar philosophy in the Negro community, and it is not surprising that the development moves from peaceful demonstration to outright civil war. The aggression of the Negro is the direct reflection of the aggression of the white community. Beneath both is commitment to a self-understanding that is the antithesis of Christian faith. But do the people know the issue that confronts them so urgently with decision? All concealment must be torn aside. All confusion between the idealistic religion of Western man and Christian faith must be dissipated. This is no merely academic issue but for our humanity a choice between the way of life and the way of death. There is no hope of peace now or ever except as the eventual fruit of the gospel of reconciliation that has been committed to our care.

Do we have to wait, then, until the world has been evangelized to know the peace of which the gospel speaks? No! The coming of the Kingdom is always by its nature the coming of God's peace. But as Paul well knew, it is not a simple peacefulness but a " peace that passes all understanding," because it is God's peace in the midst of a world that contradicts God's will. We cannot for a moment close our eyes to the contradiction and the conflict either in our world or in ourselves. To conceal from ourselves that there is still in us and in the community for which we are responsible much that still resists the will of God and must be conquered, and thereby to procure for ourselves a specious and tenuous peace of mind, is folly. And yet there is

a peace, like a great rock beneath our feet, that God provides for us when once his mercy and his love in Jesus
Christ have flooded in upon us and our lives are unconditionally in his hand, open to his truth and open for him to
work his will in us. Our peace is founded not on anything
in ourselves but on the promise revealed to us in Jesus
Christ of what God purposes to make of us and of our
humanity.

Postscript

To DO what it sets out to do, this book should perhaps have been cast in dialogue form, letting representatives of the common man appear and express for themselves what meaning key Christian words have for them. The redefining of the words would then have gradually proceeded in a conversational give-and-take. It was in conversations of that kind that I became acutely aware of how a whole new understanding of the Bible and the Christian faith can open up to people when someone takes the trouble to sit down with them and help them get free of the false meanings which have become attached to the words. I would like to have been able to put on paper a reproduction of a series of such conversations. But to write dialogue that lives is a literary art and a capacity which few possess. So I have done what seemed to be the next best thing: I have written brief essays which gather together in condensed form the substance of such conversations. It may be that in the process of condensation what was simple and clear in the form of conversation has become opaque and difficult. My fondest hope would therefore be that these chapters might become a stimulus and starting point for new conversations in which what has been condensed here would be allowed to open out and become only a guide toward exploration of Christian meanings.

Perhaps a word may be said in defense of expecting of the reader a quality of thinking that is both strenuous and critical. I am convinced that the church has erred in the past by trying to make Christian truth so simple that it has frequently only succeeded in making it so superficial that it is innocuous. The church has not been sufficiently a place where men and women are challenged and provoked to think. Some years ago I wrote a book on the implications of the Apostles' Creed for Christian education, with church school teachers in mind as my audience, and I ventured to use several of the chapters as lectures at a conference of ministers and seminary students. I was a little fearful that they might think my language not sufficiently professional for them. But at a reception following one lecture a young minister expressed his reaction in these terms: " This is great stuff for us ministers, but how do we get it down to the level of our people? " I tried as gently as possible to suggest that the problem is not one of simplification but rather one of speaking without loss of integrity or profundity in the language of the hearers. To lose the integrity or the depth of meaning is to have lost all, so that the speaking no longer has any purpose. Therefore I trust that readers who find some passages not as simple as the term " ABC's " had led them to expect will recognize that it is the depth of the questions in which we are all of us involved that forbids a simplicity that would be superficial.